DIESES BUCH
Gehört

SKYSCRAPERS MALBUCH

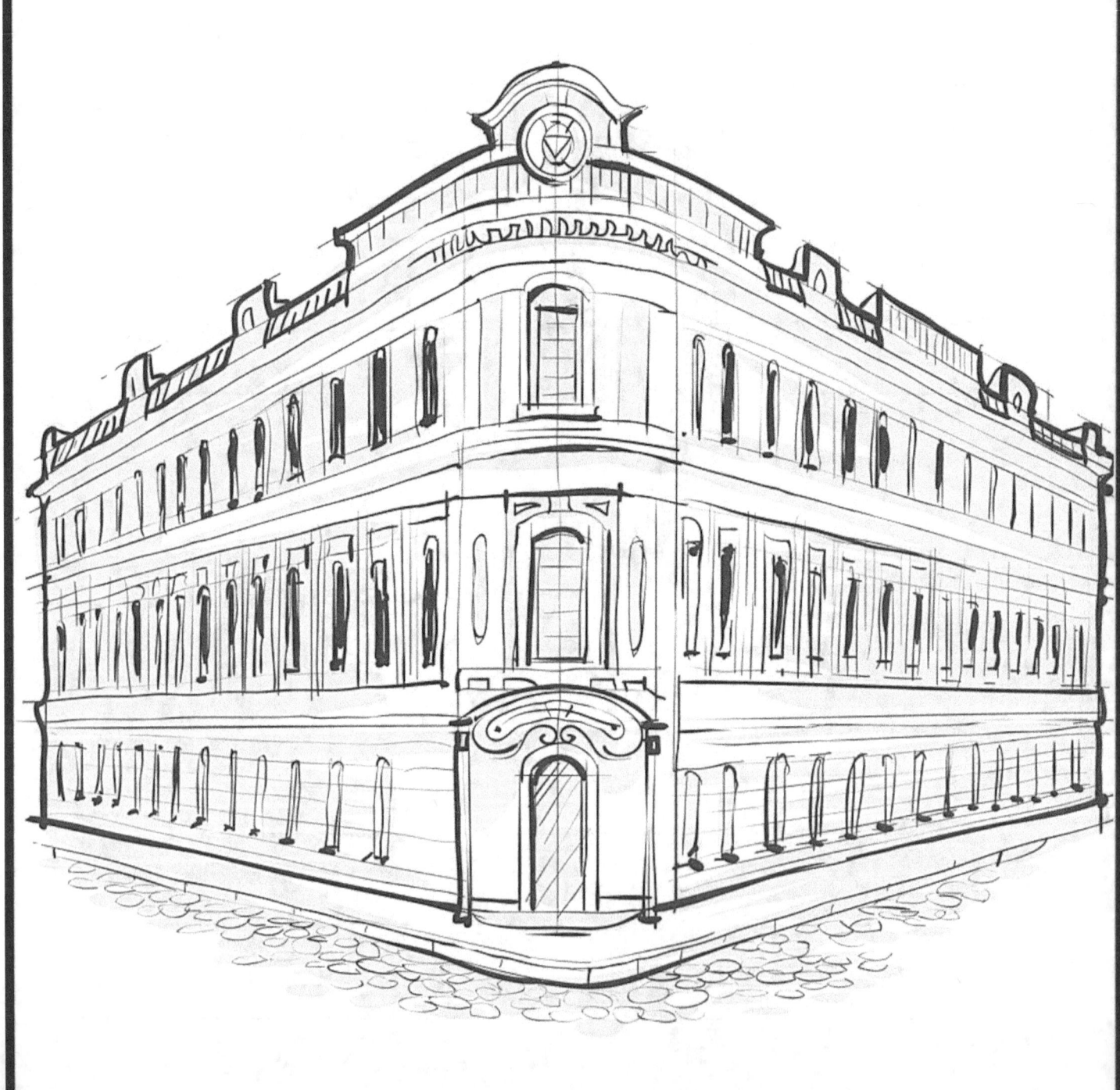

SKYSCRAPERS MALBUCH

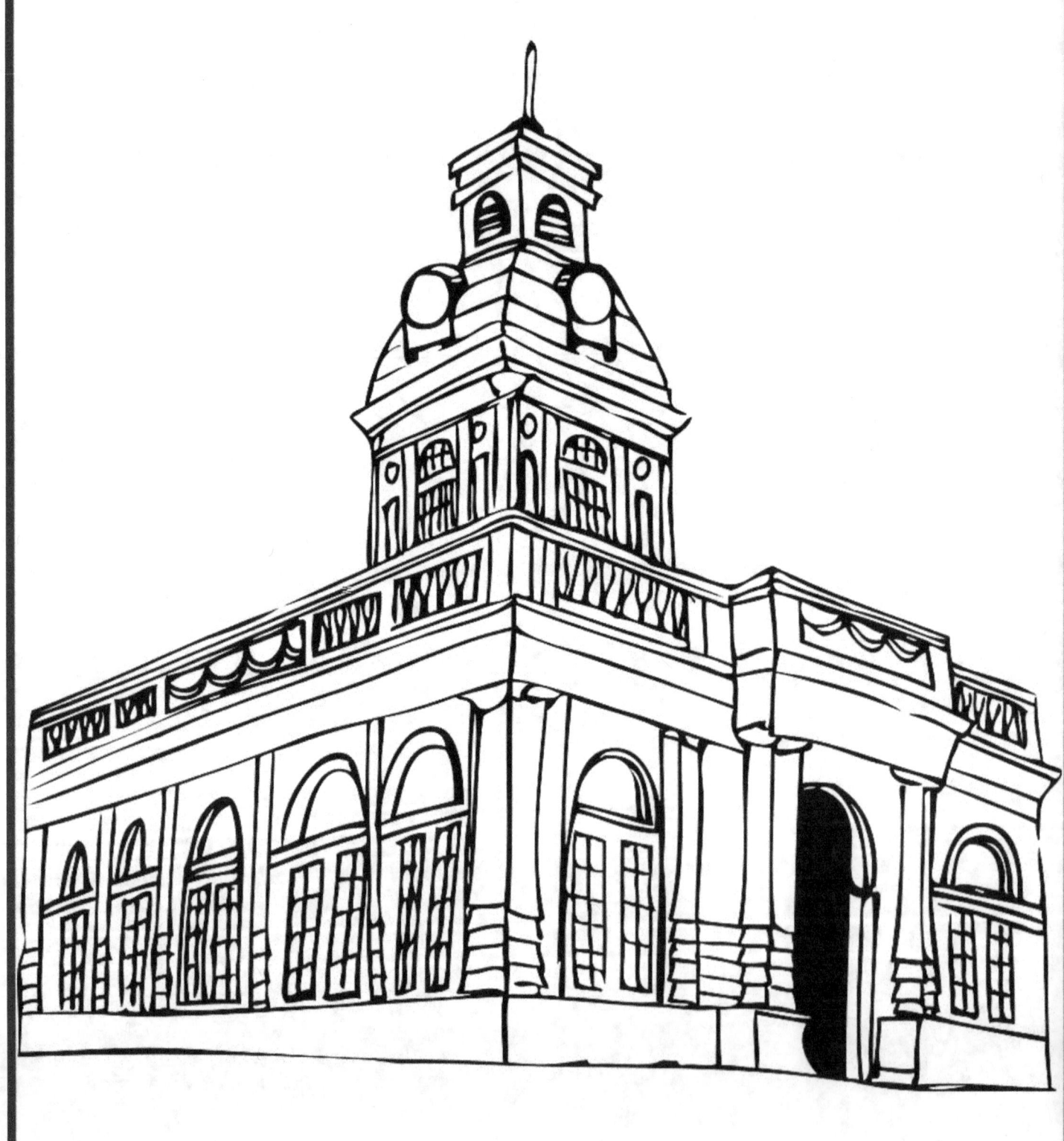

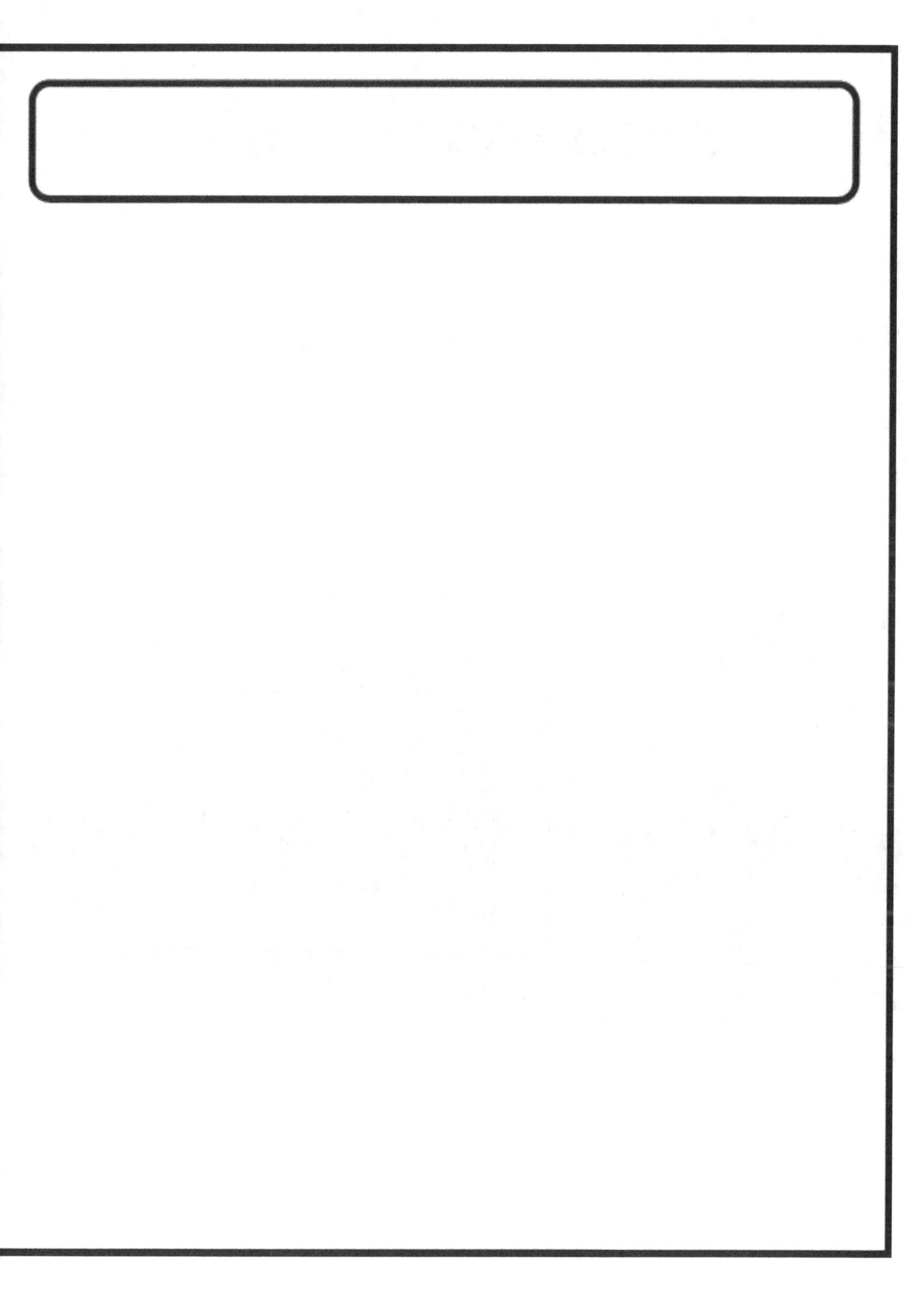

SKYSCRAPERS MALBUCH

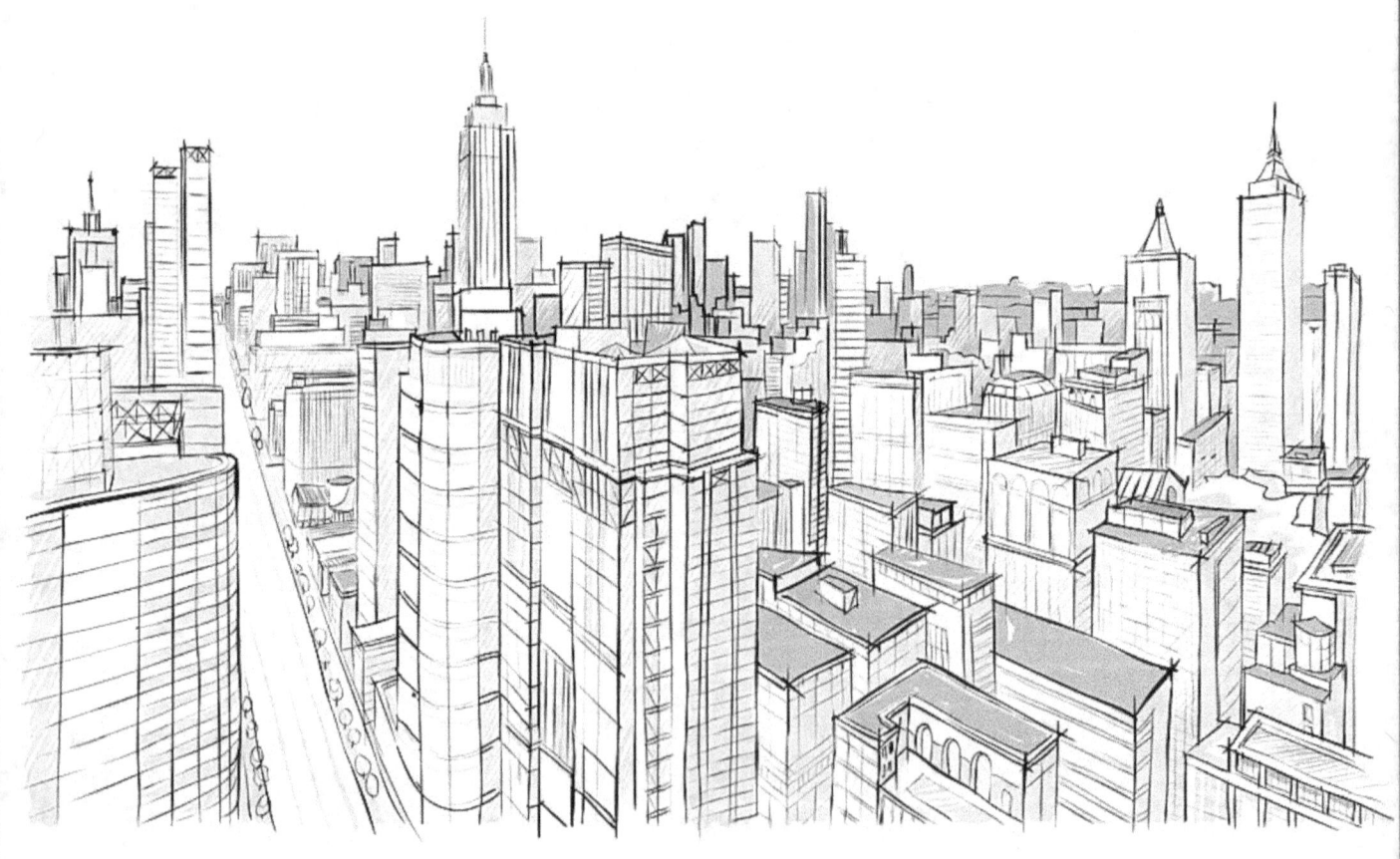

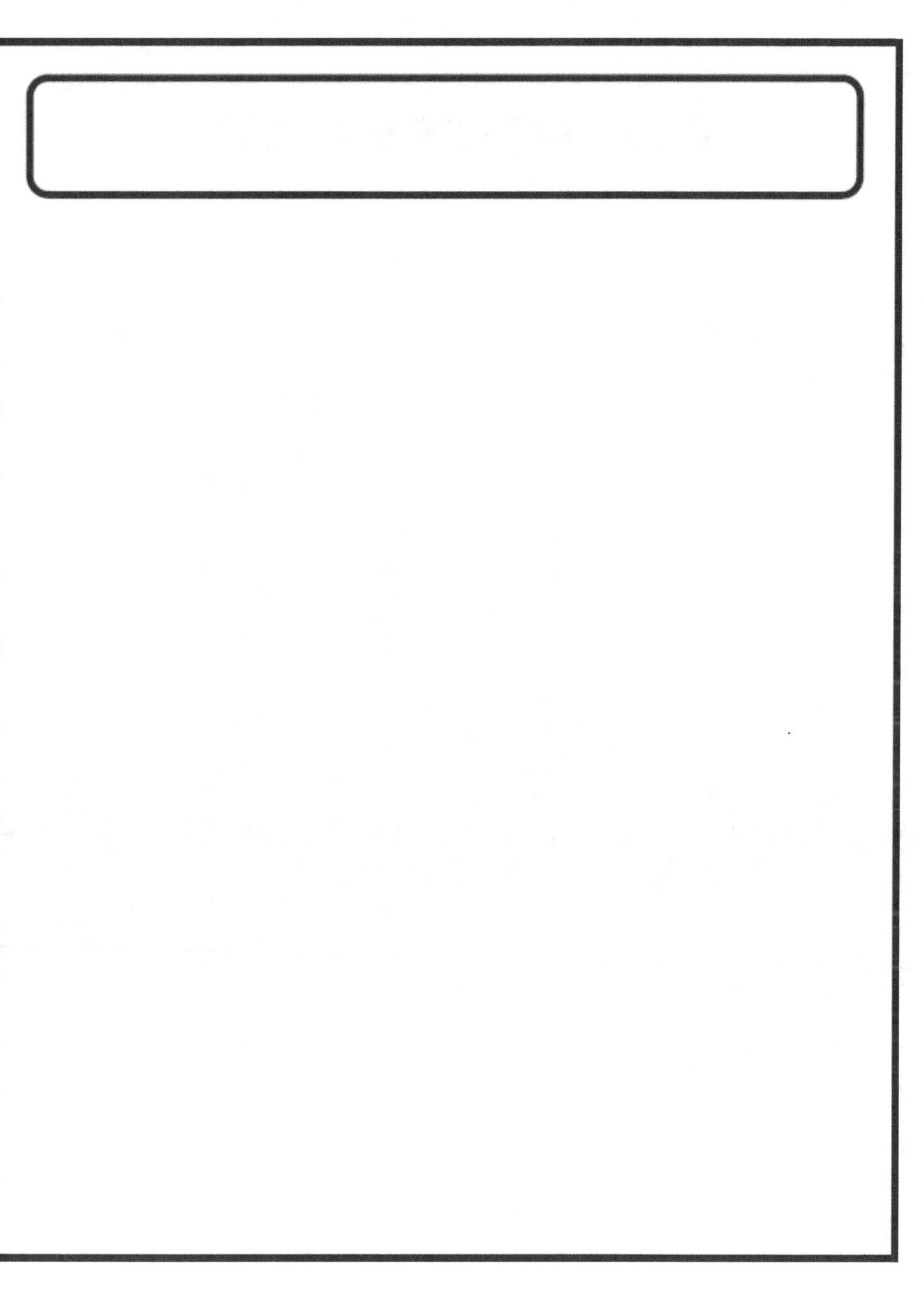

SKYSCRAPERS MALBUCH

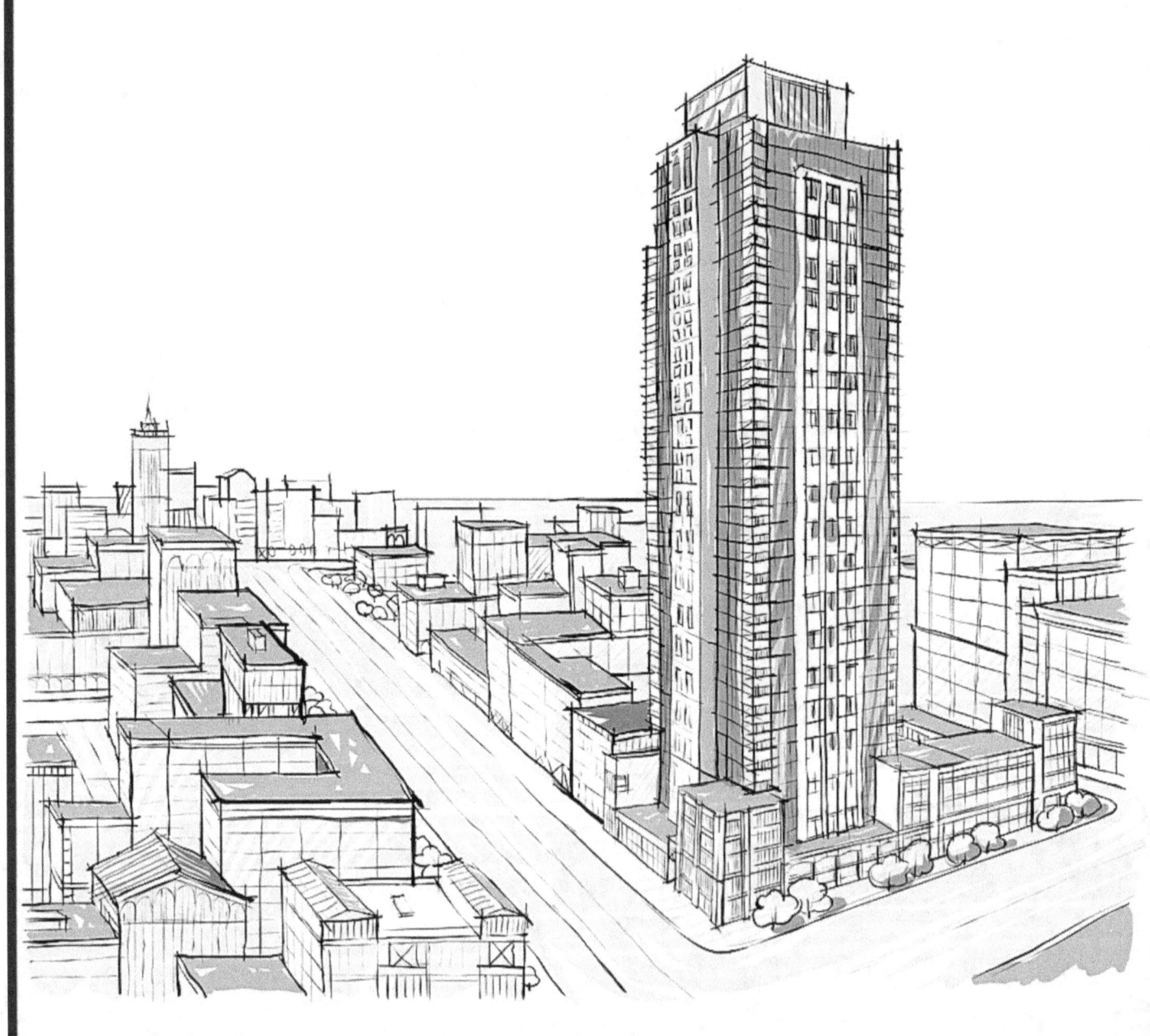

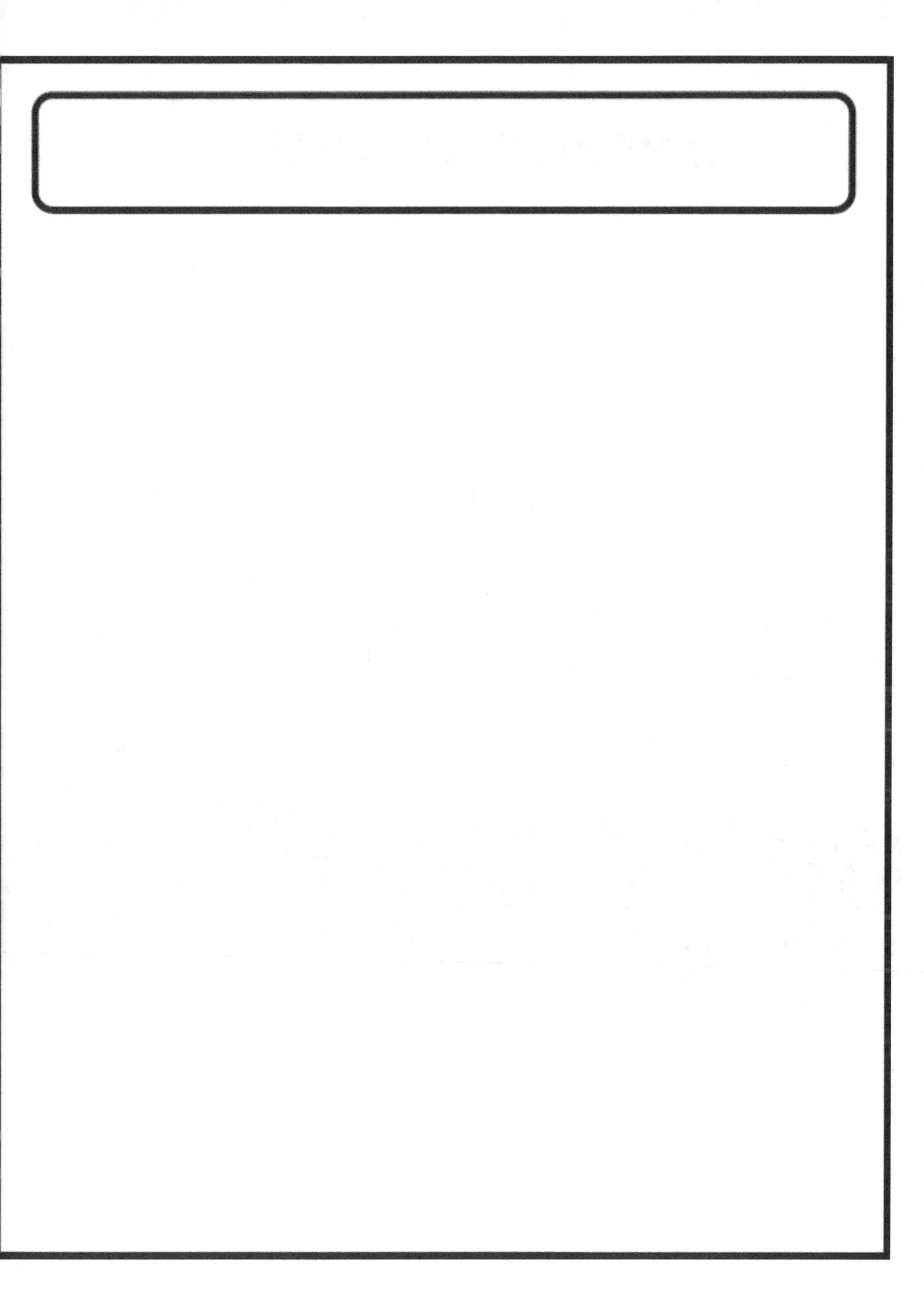

SKYSCRAPERS MALBUCH

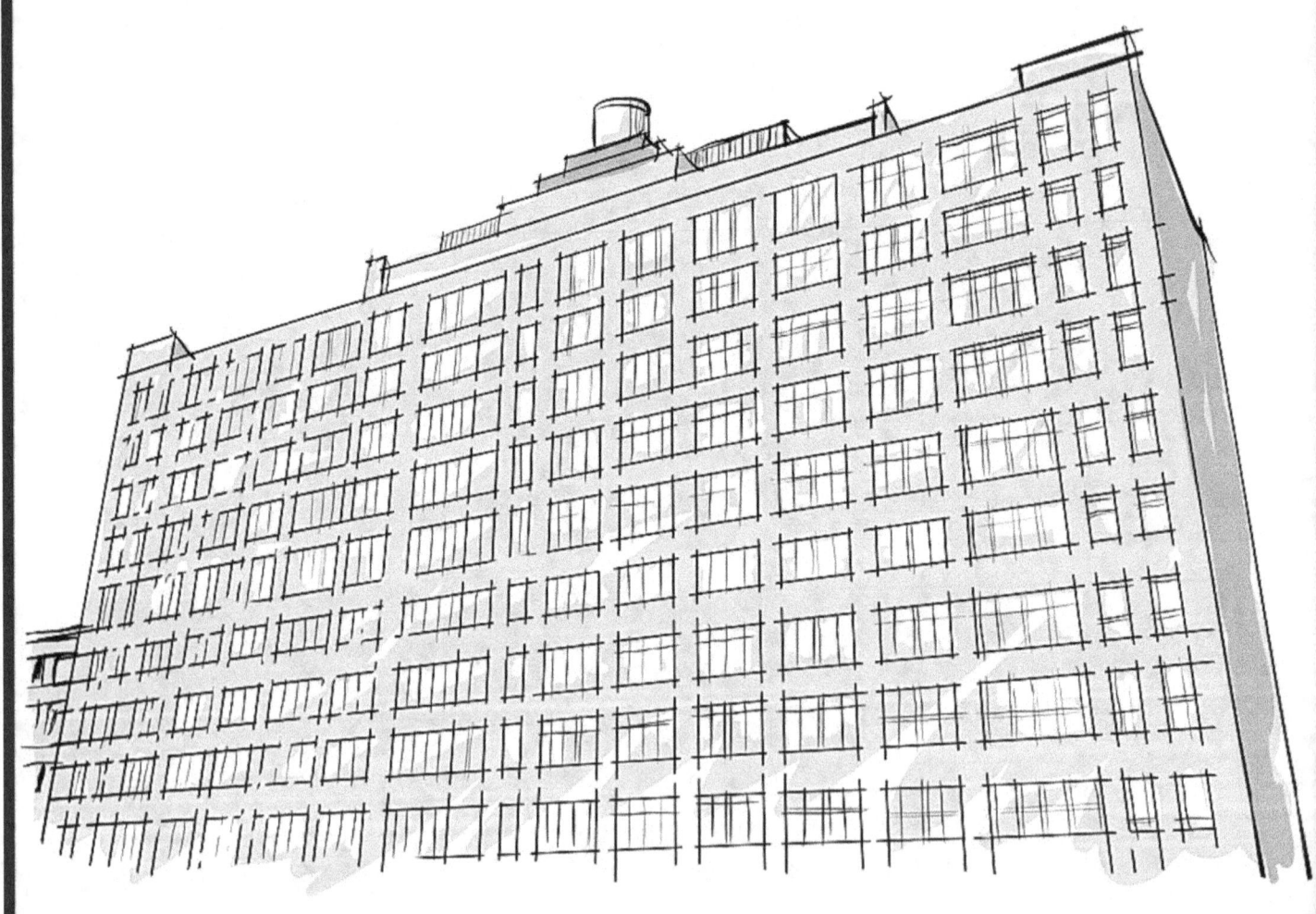

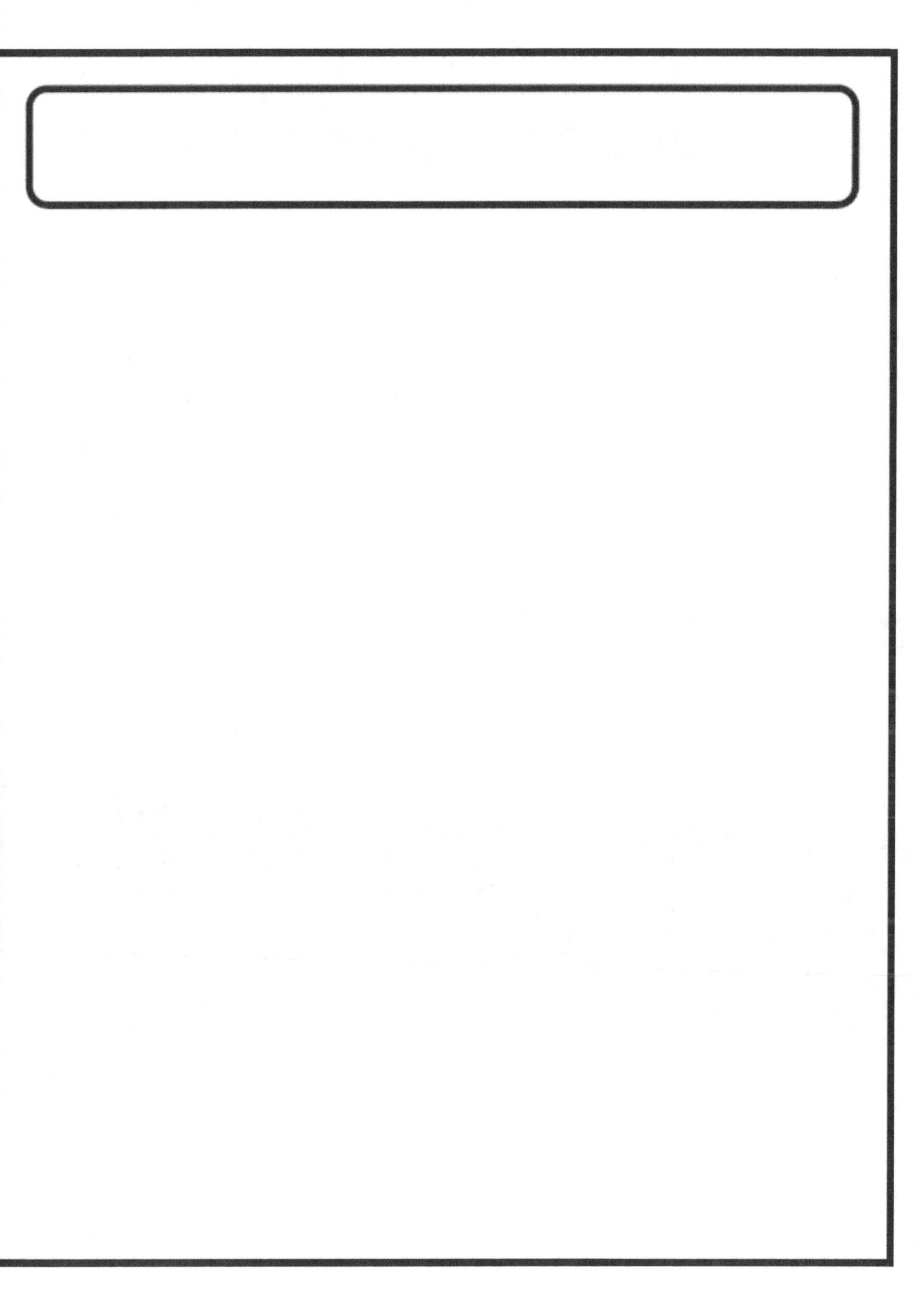

SKYSCRAPERS MALBUCH

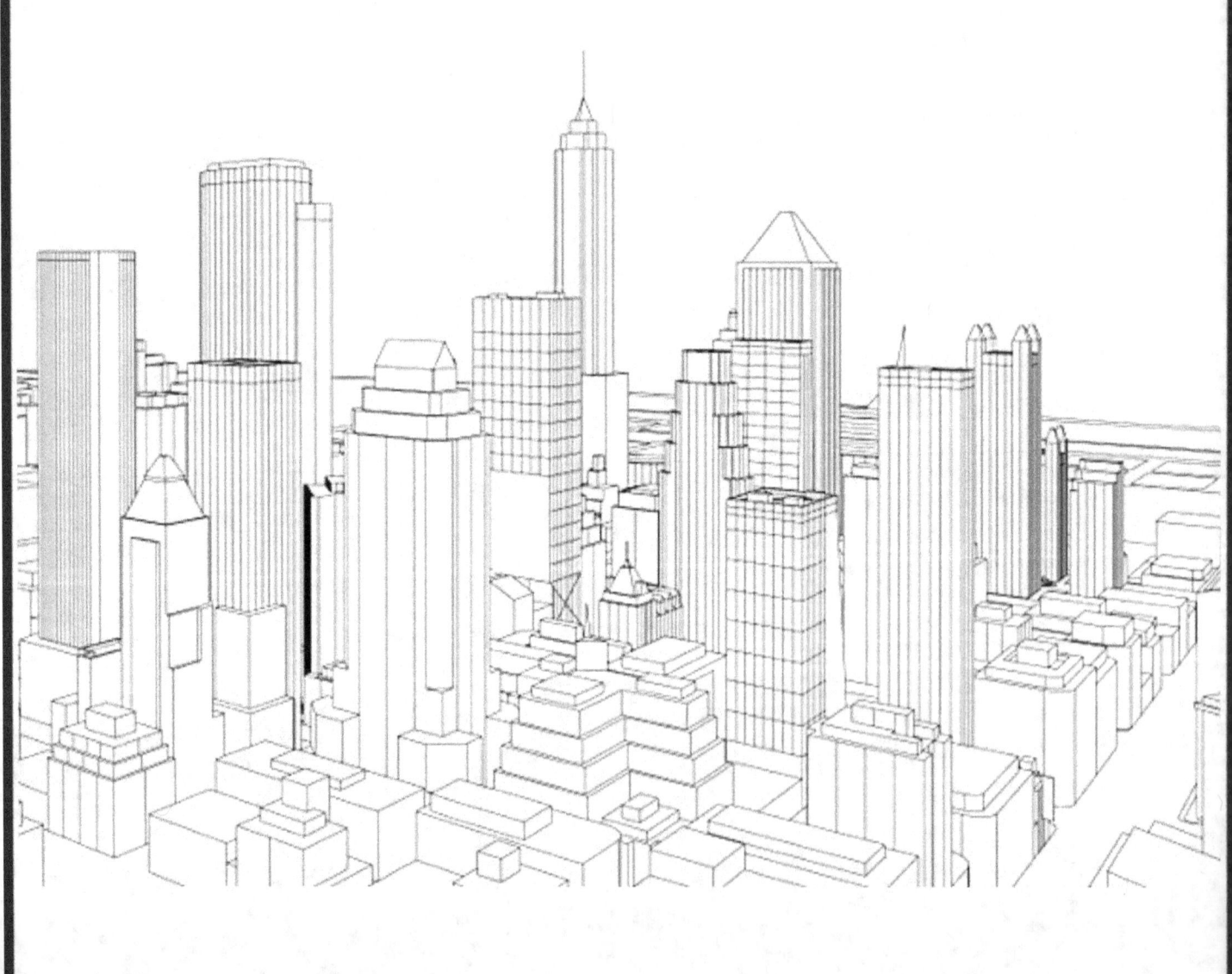

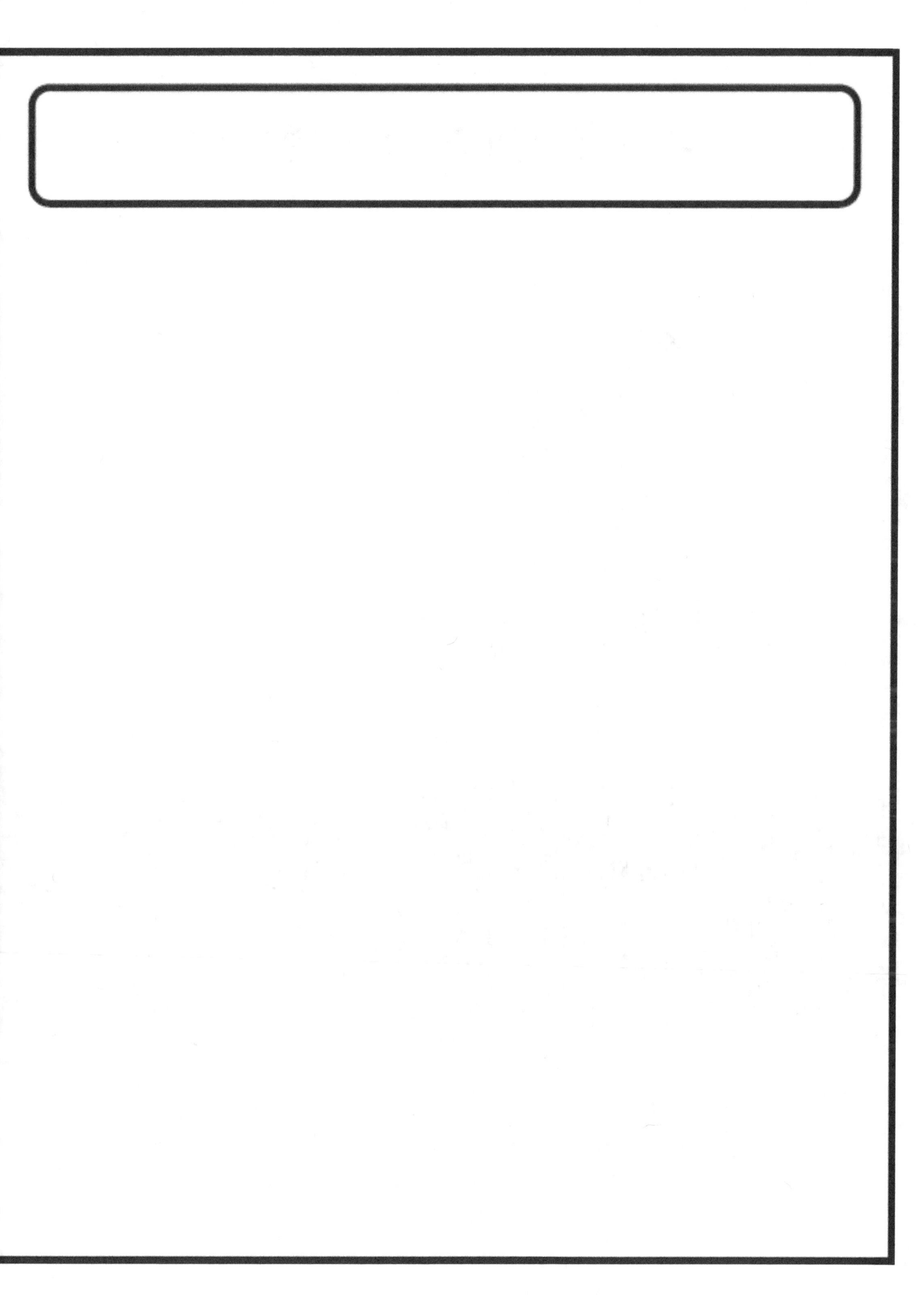

SKYSCRAPERS MALBUCH

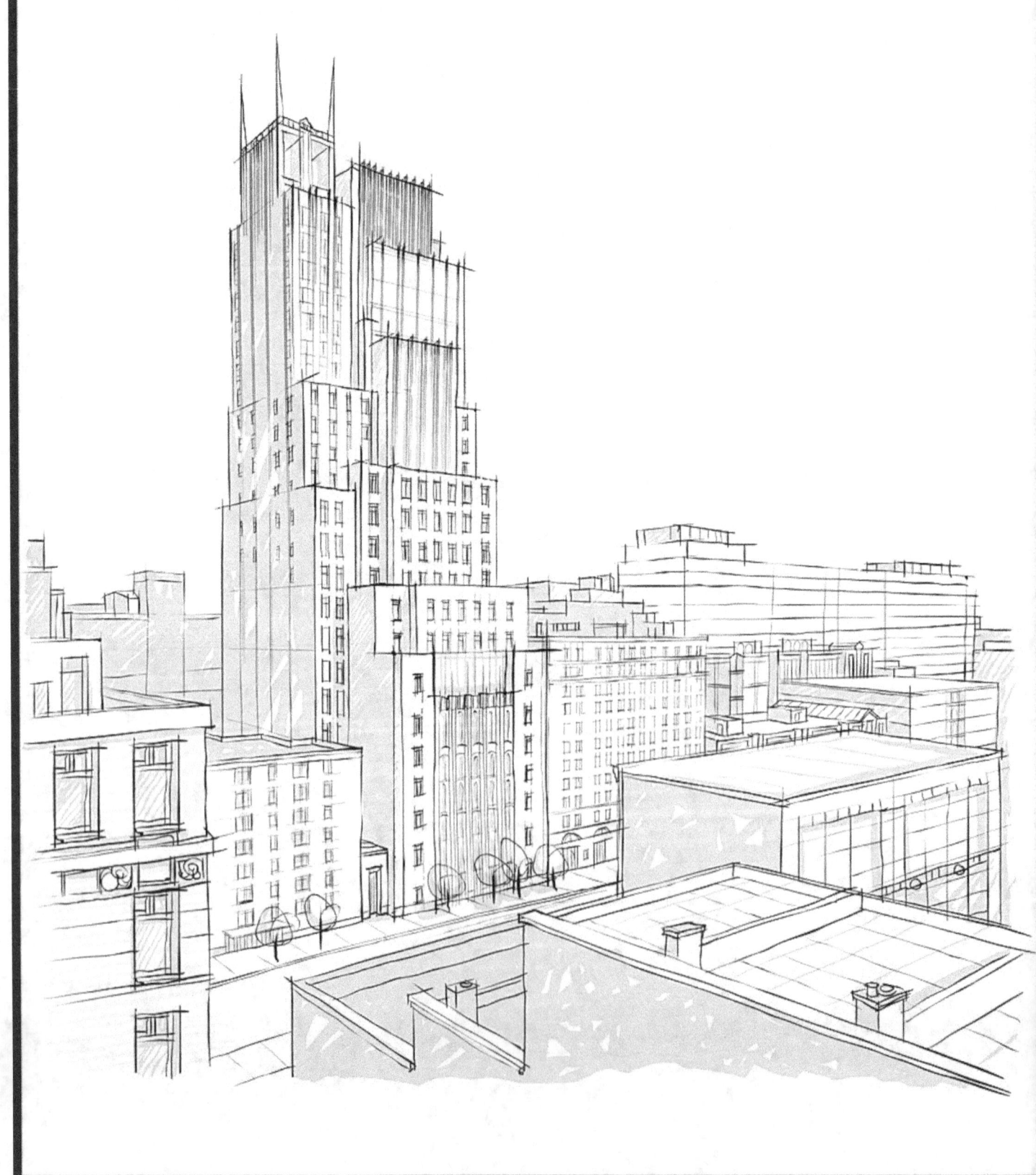

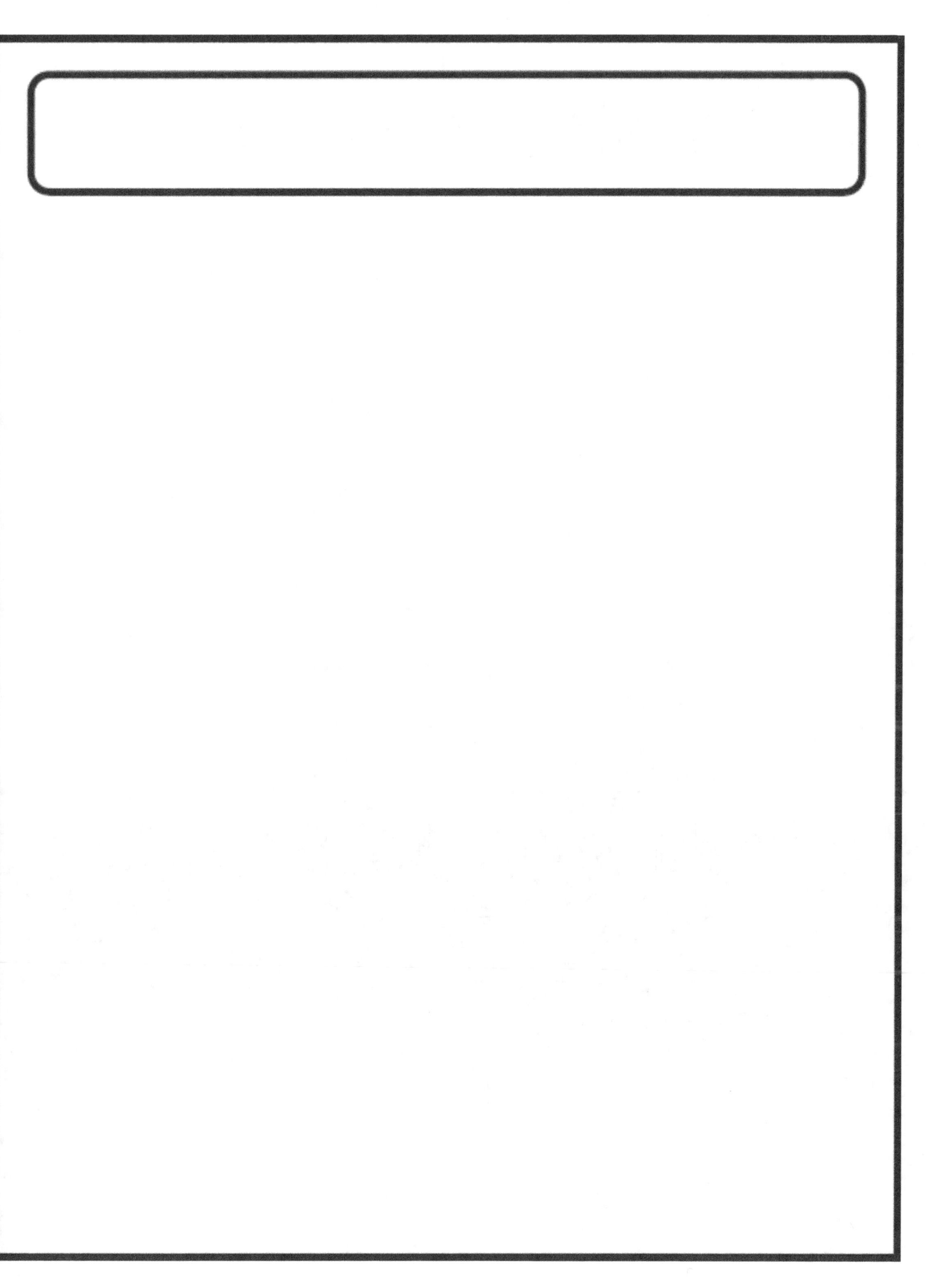

SKYSCRAPERS MALBUCH

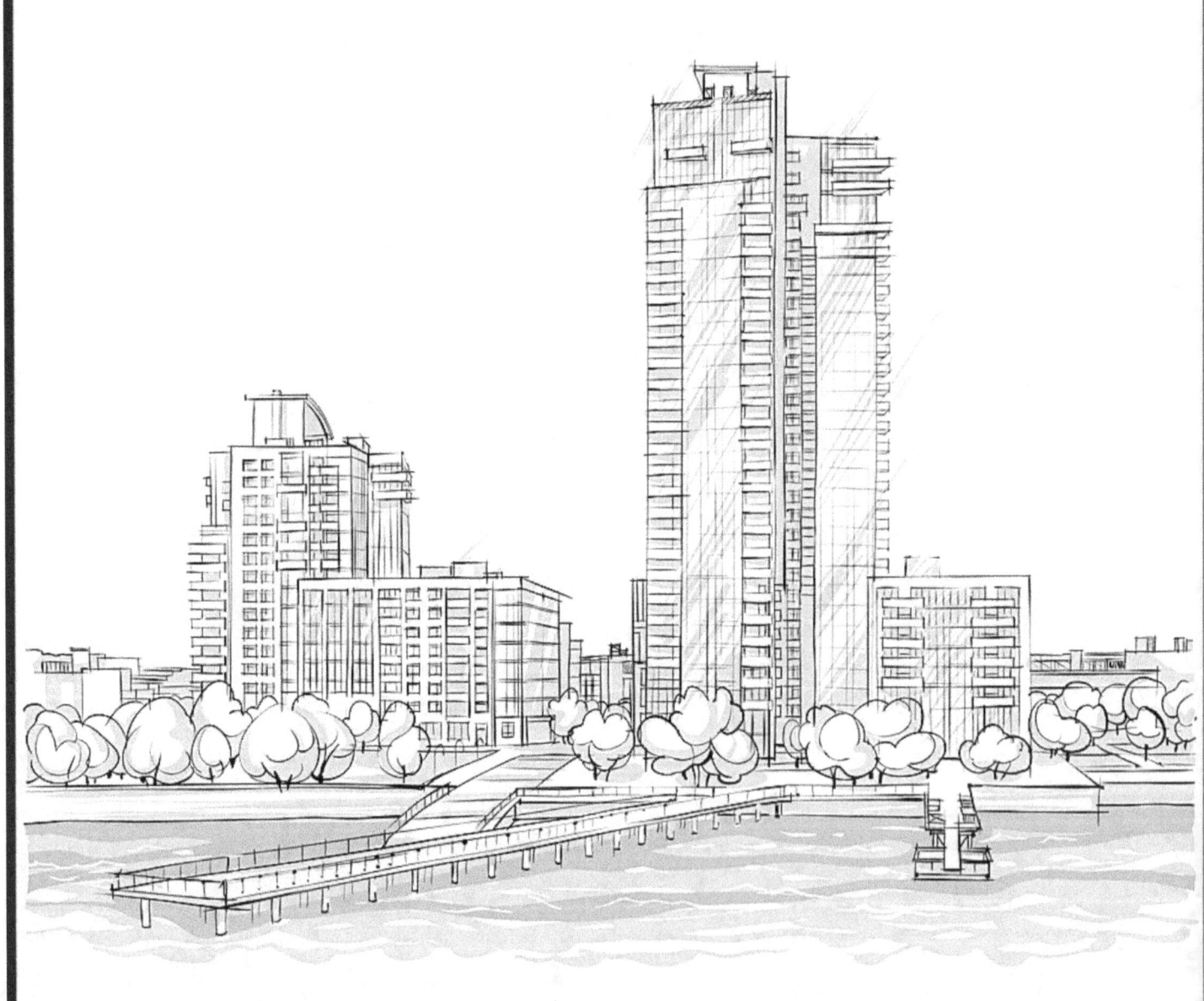

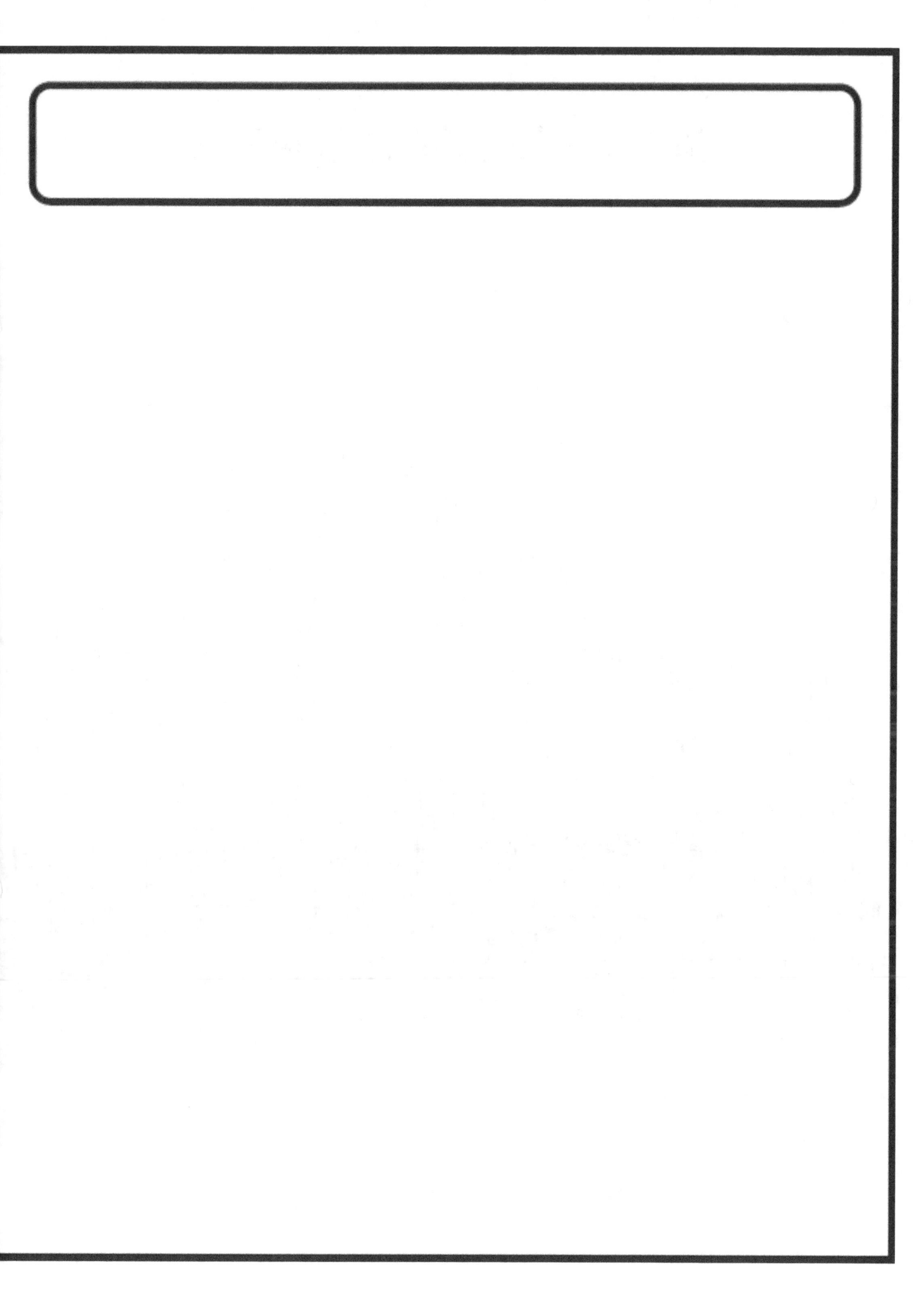

SKYSCRAPERS MALBUCH

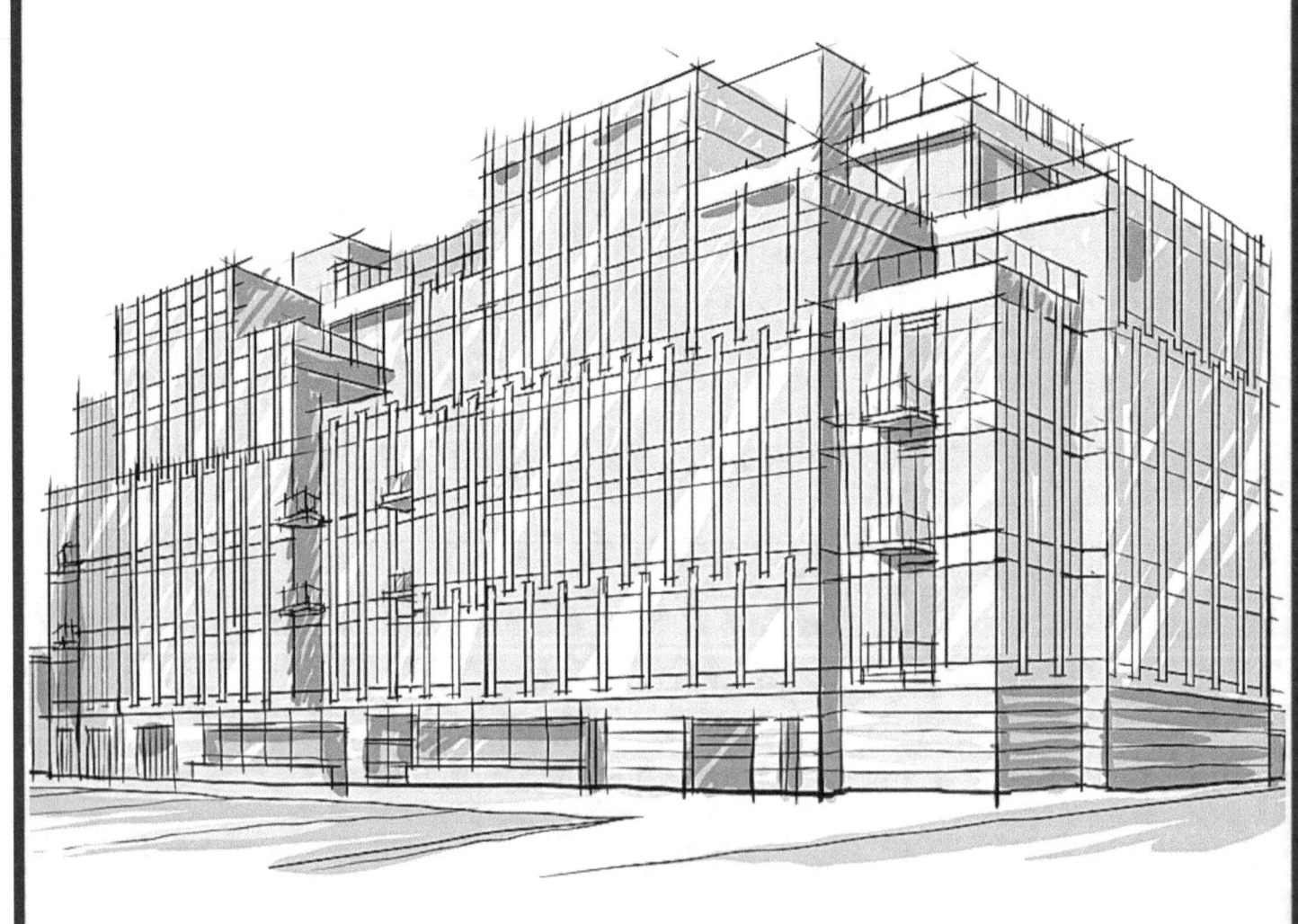

SKYSCRAPERS MALBUCH

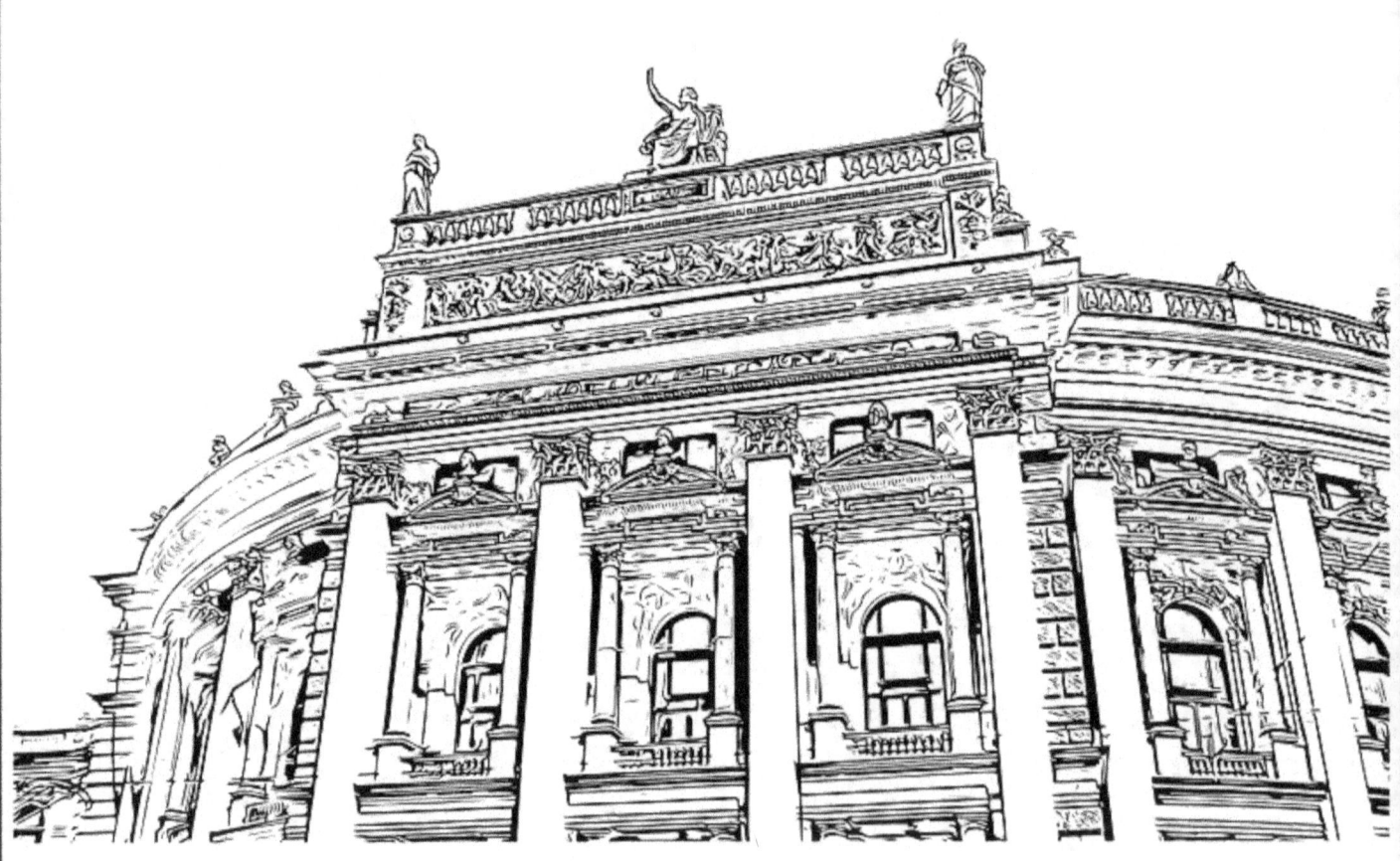

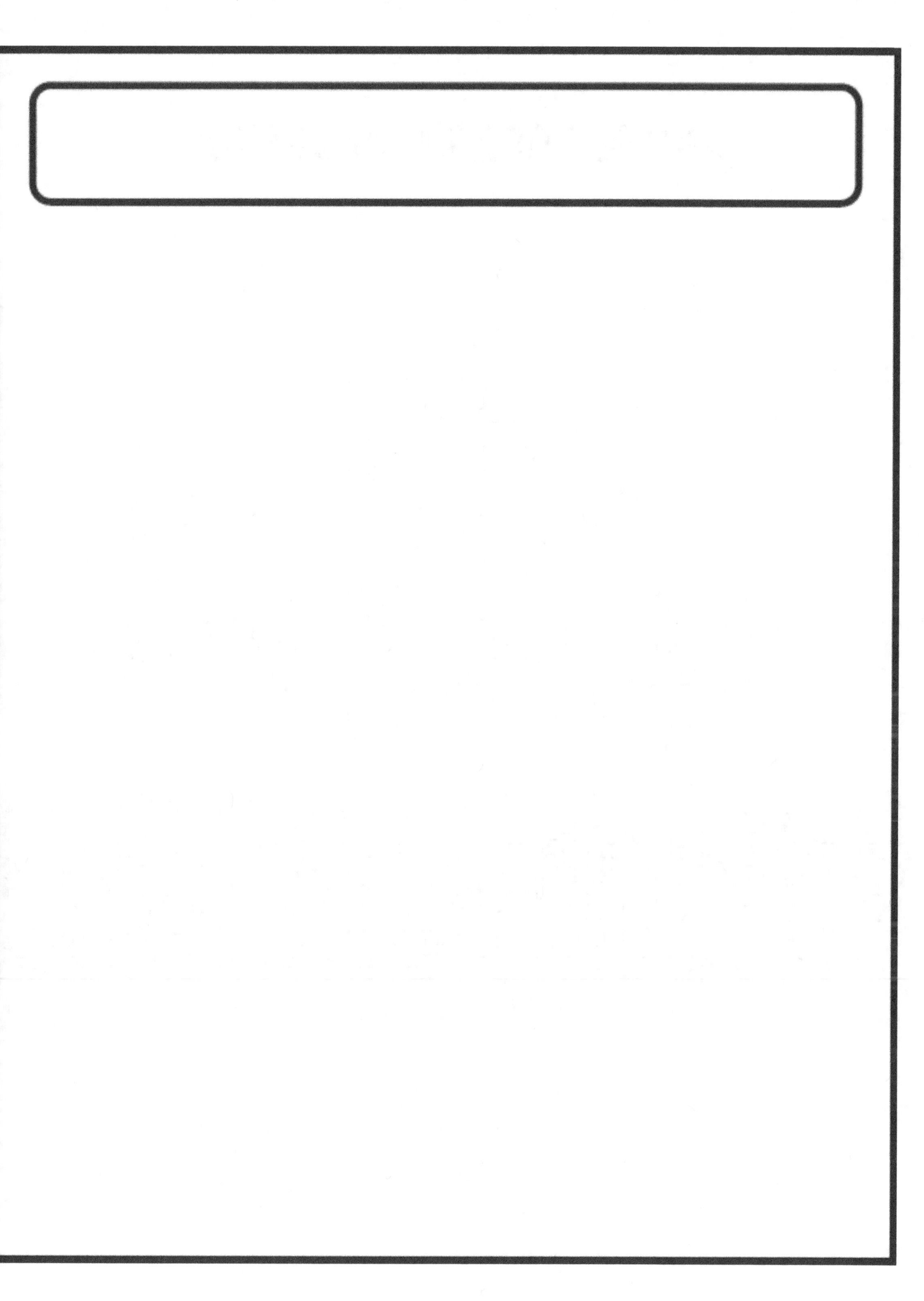

SKYSCRAPERS MALBUCH

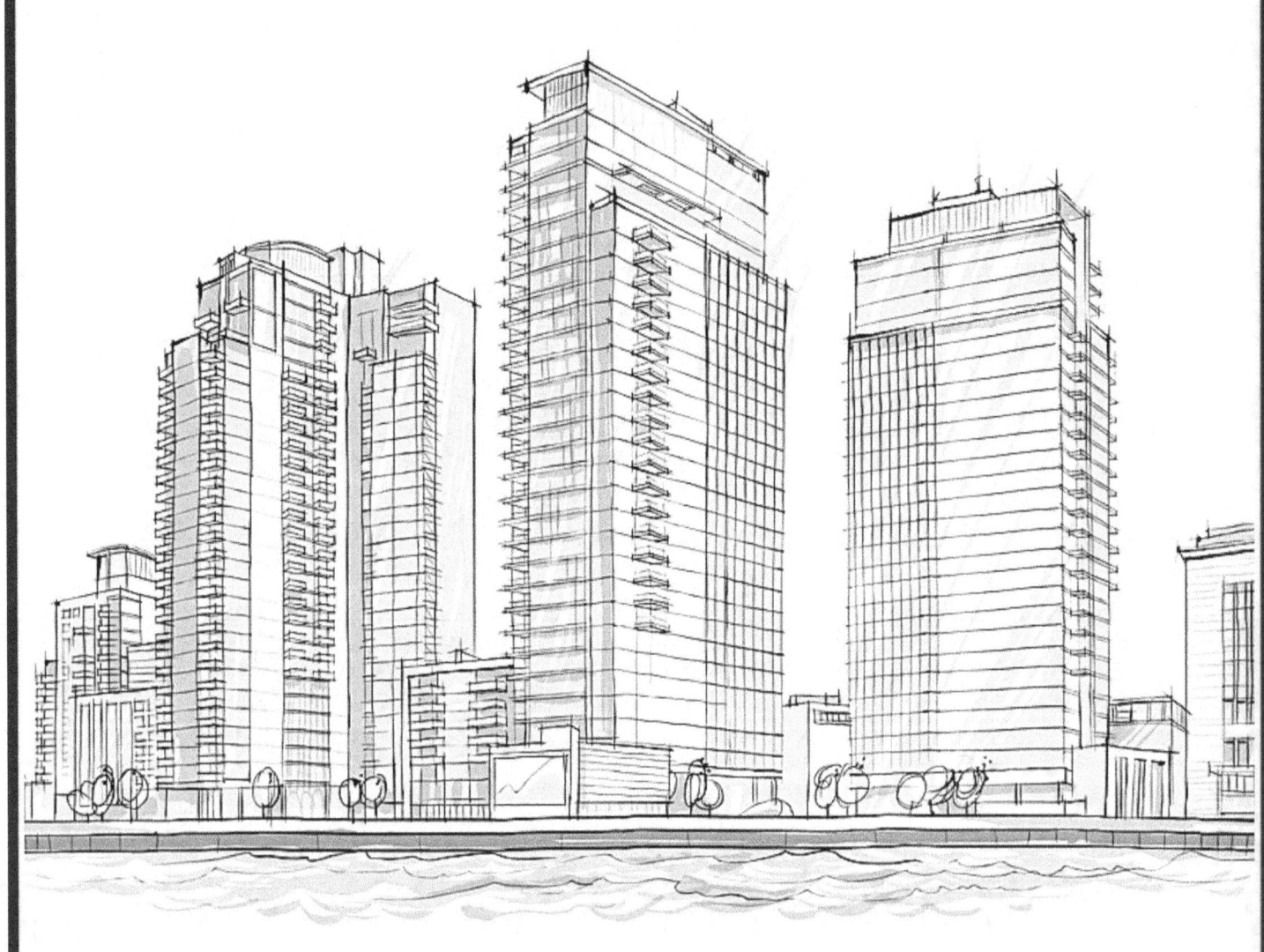

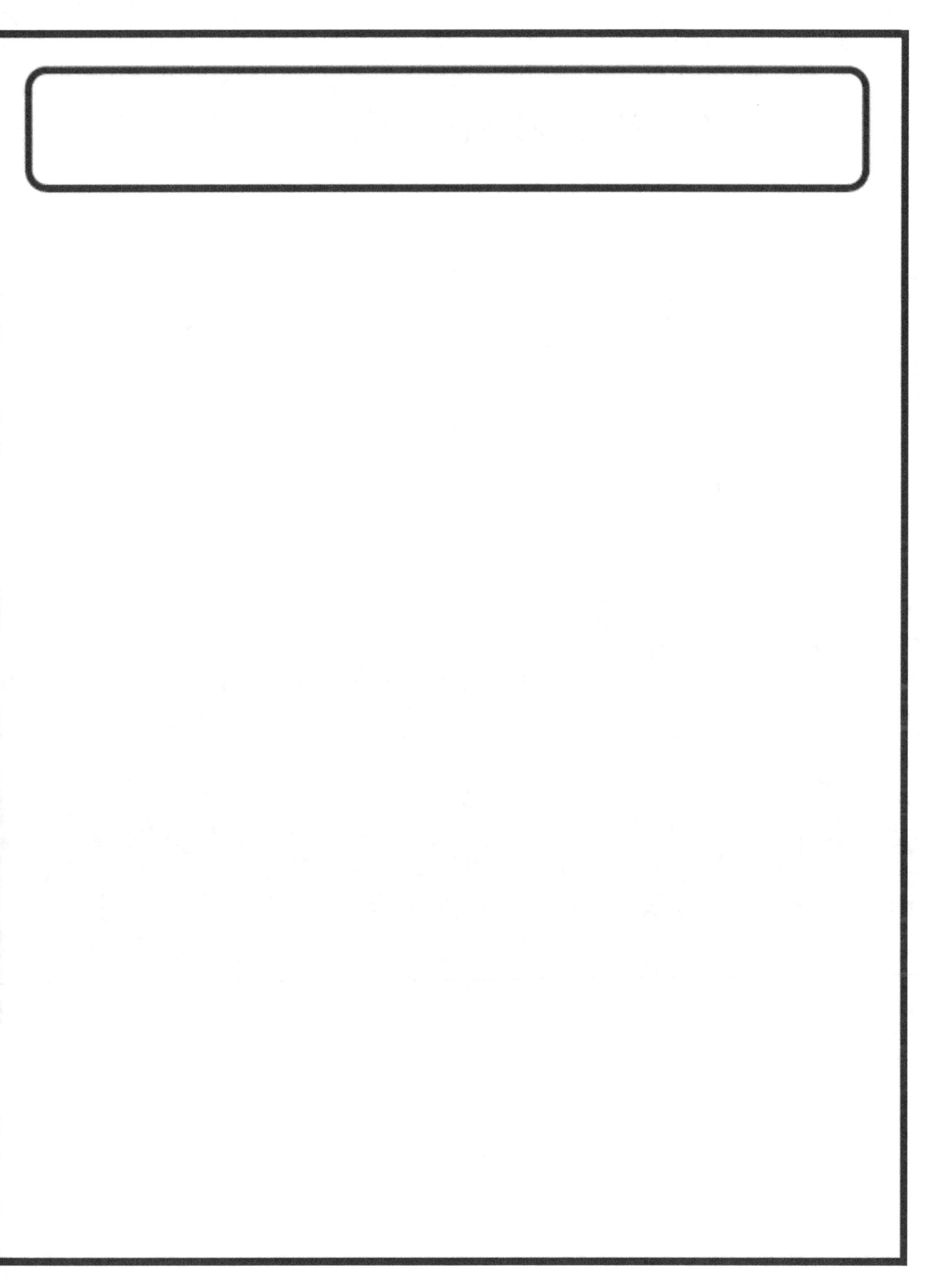

SKYSCRAPERS MALBUCH

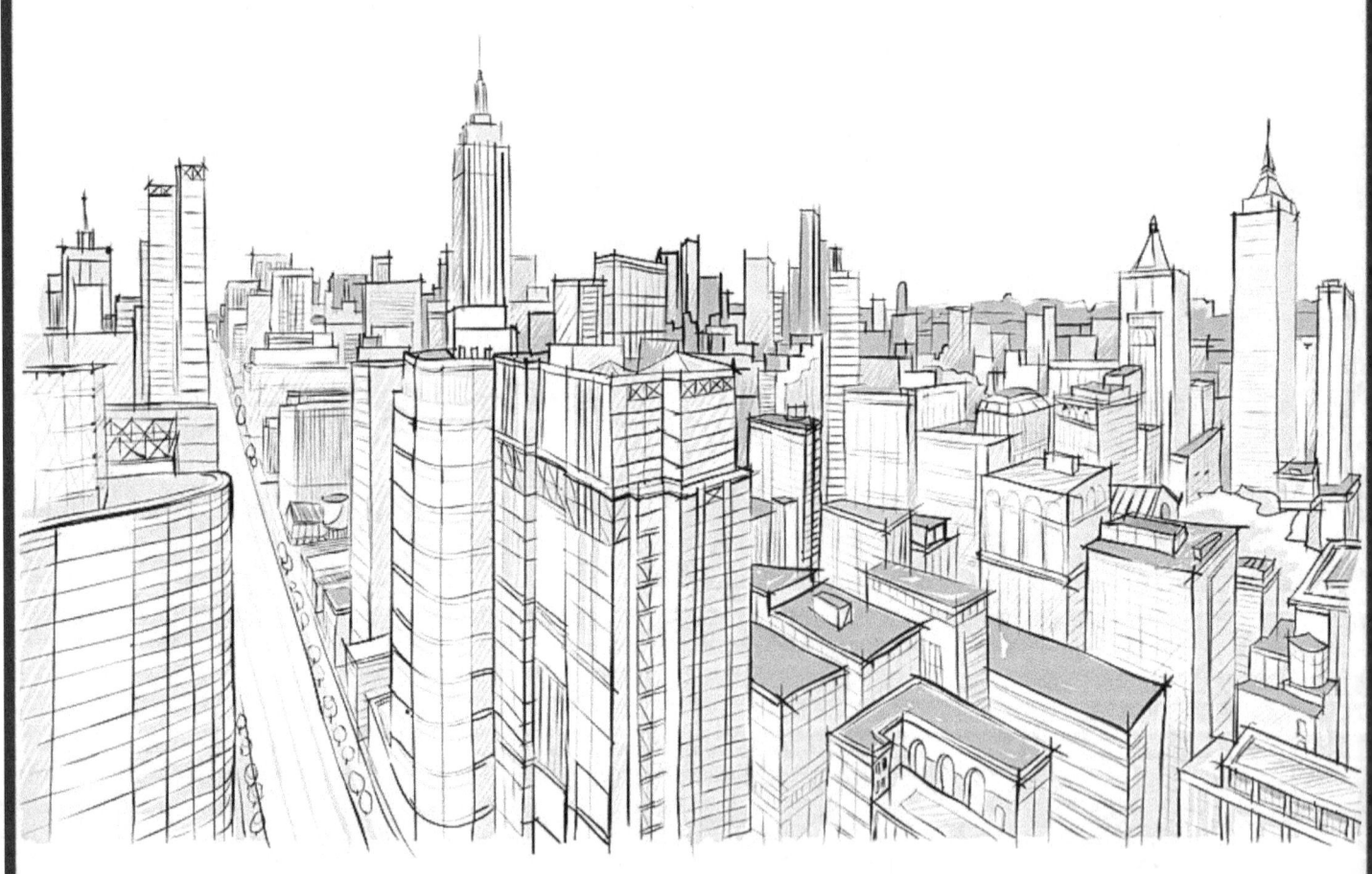

SKYSCRAPERS MALBUCH

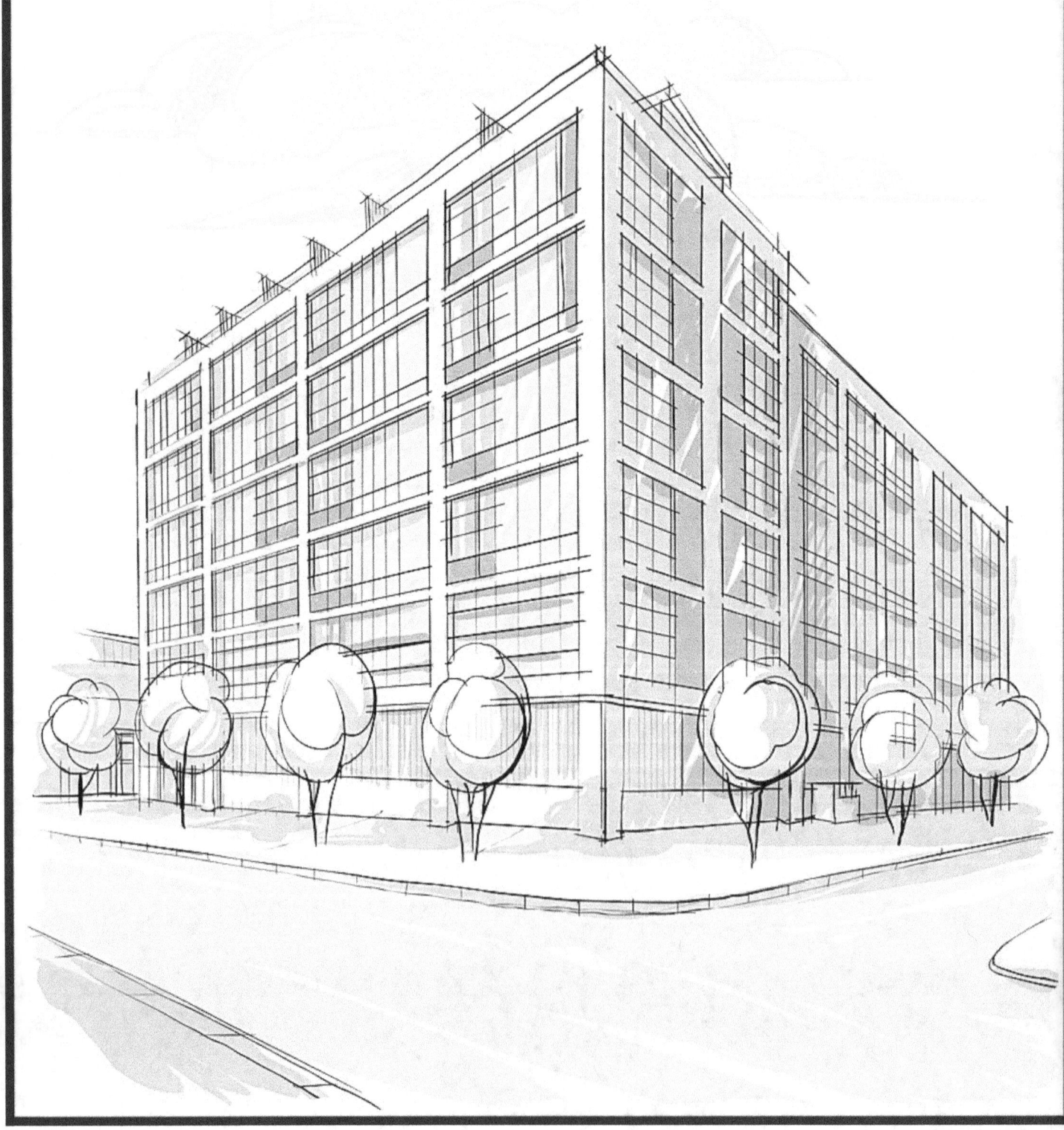

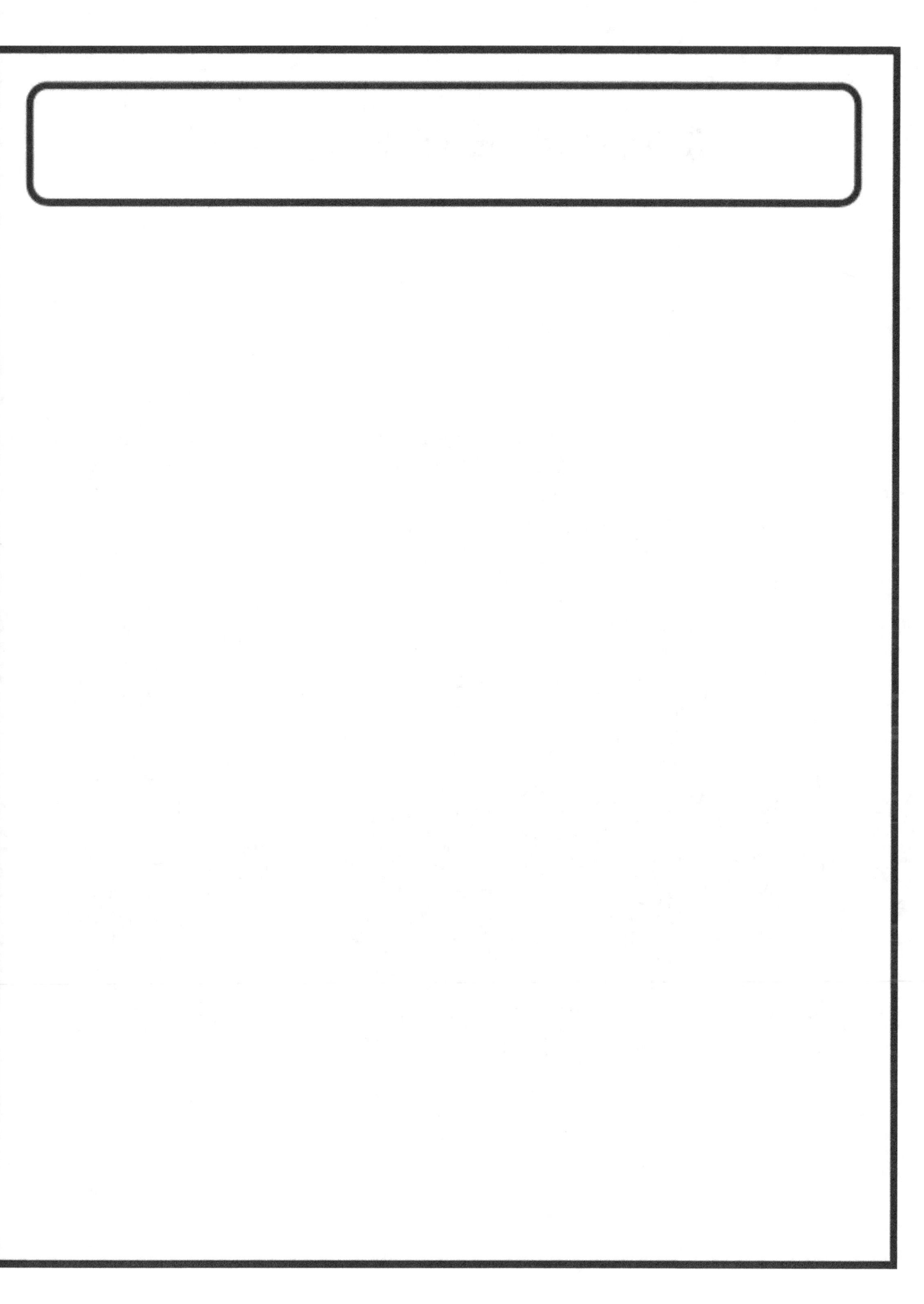

SKYSCRAPERS MALBUCH

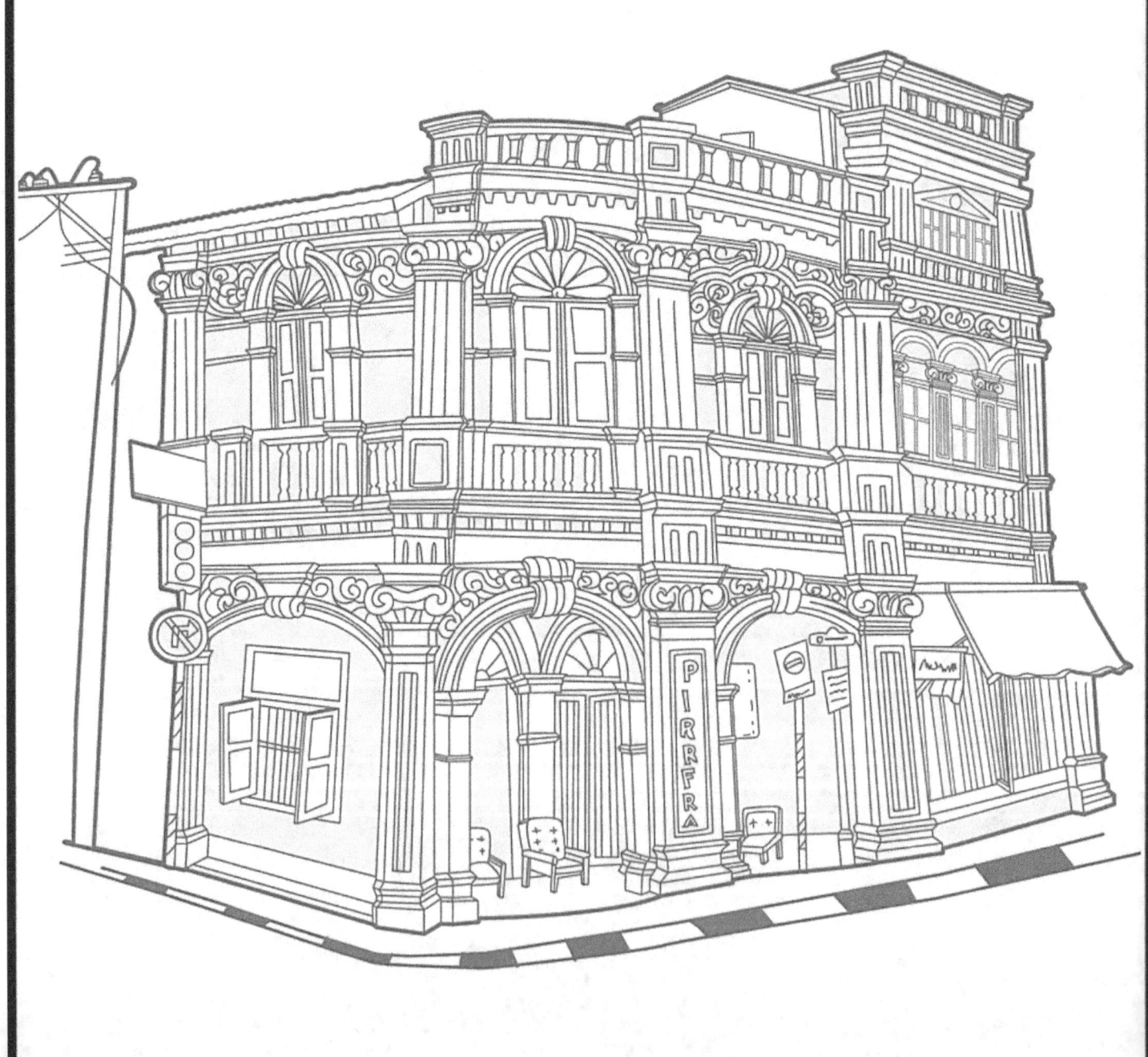

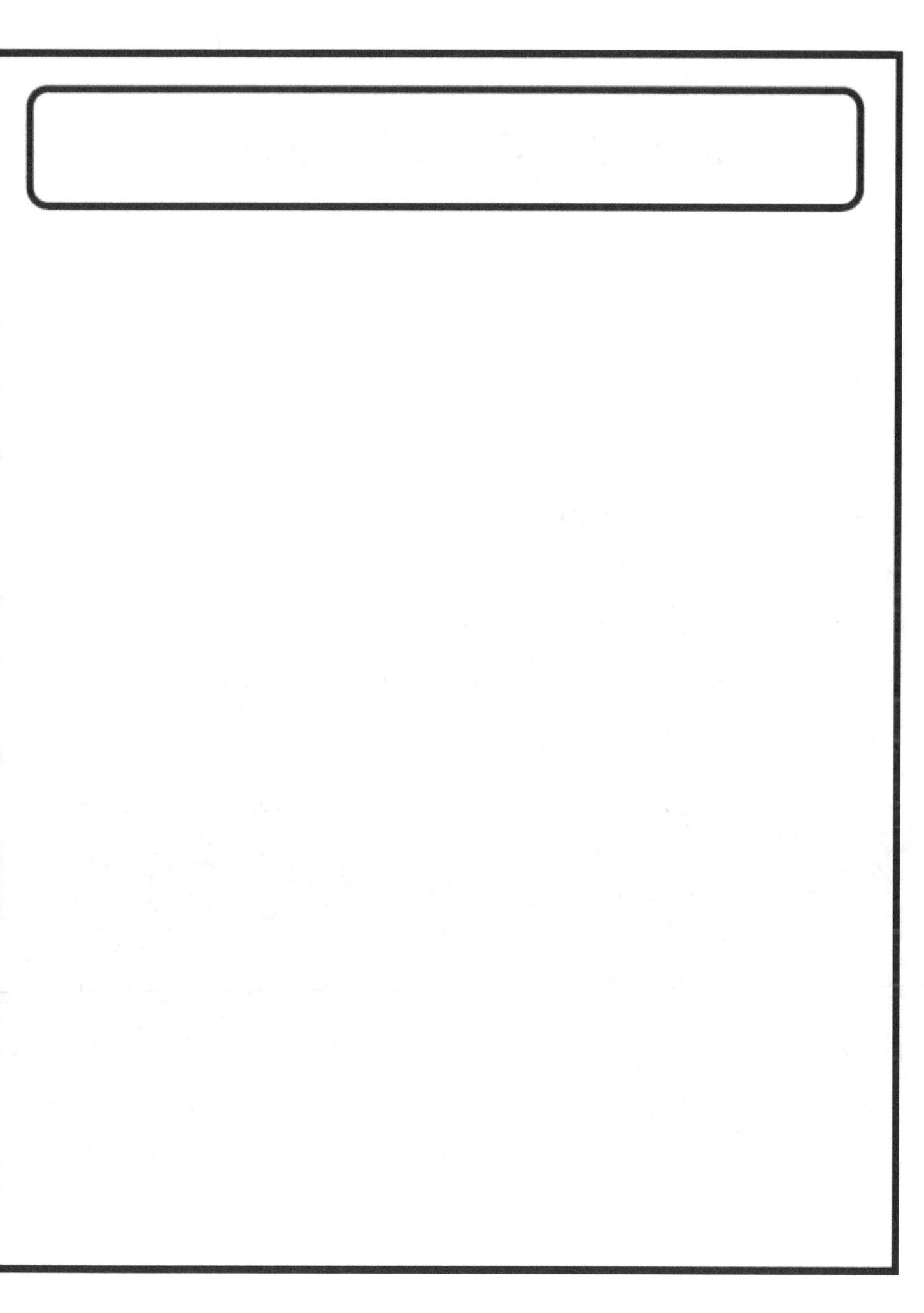

SKYSCRAPERS MALBUCH

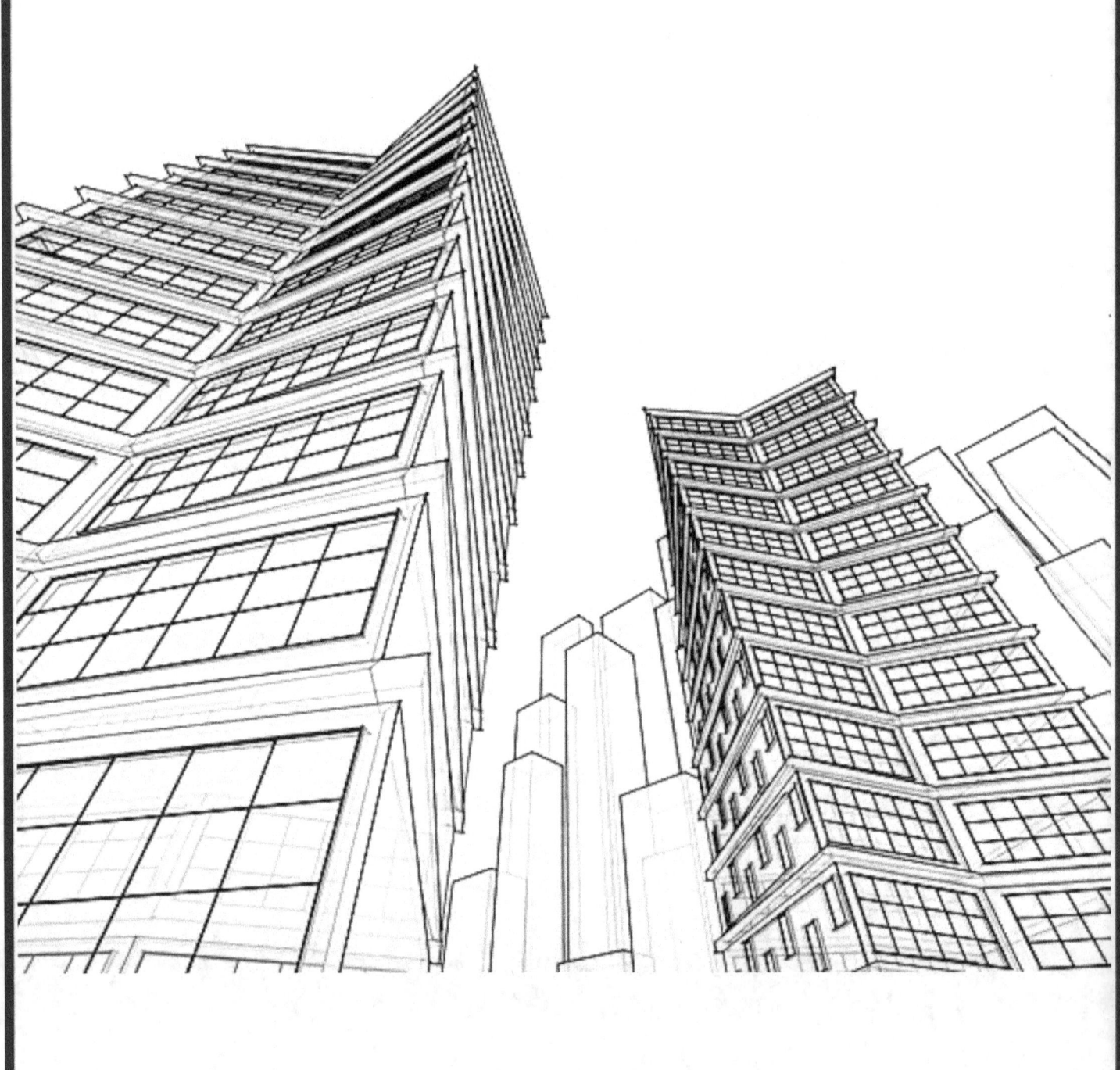

SKYSCRAPERS MALBUCH

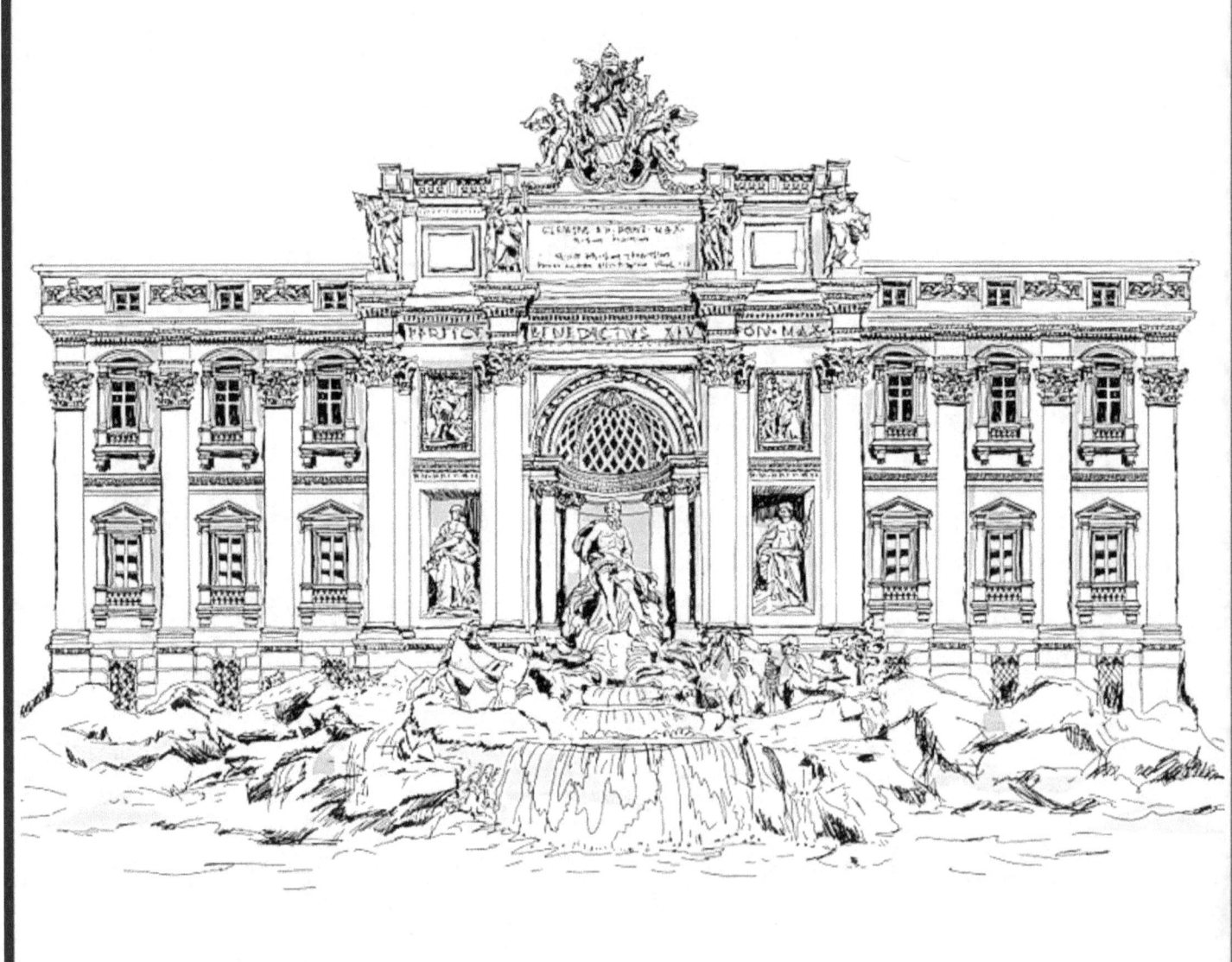

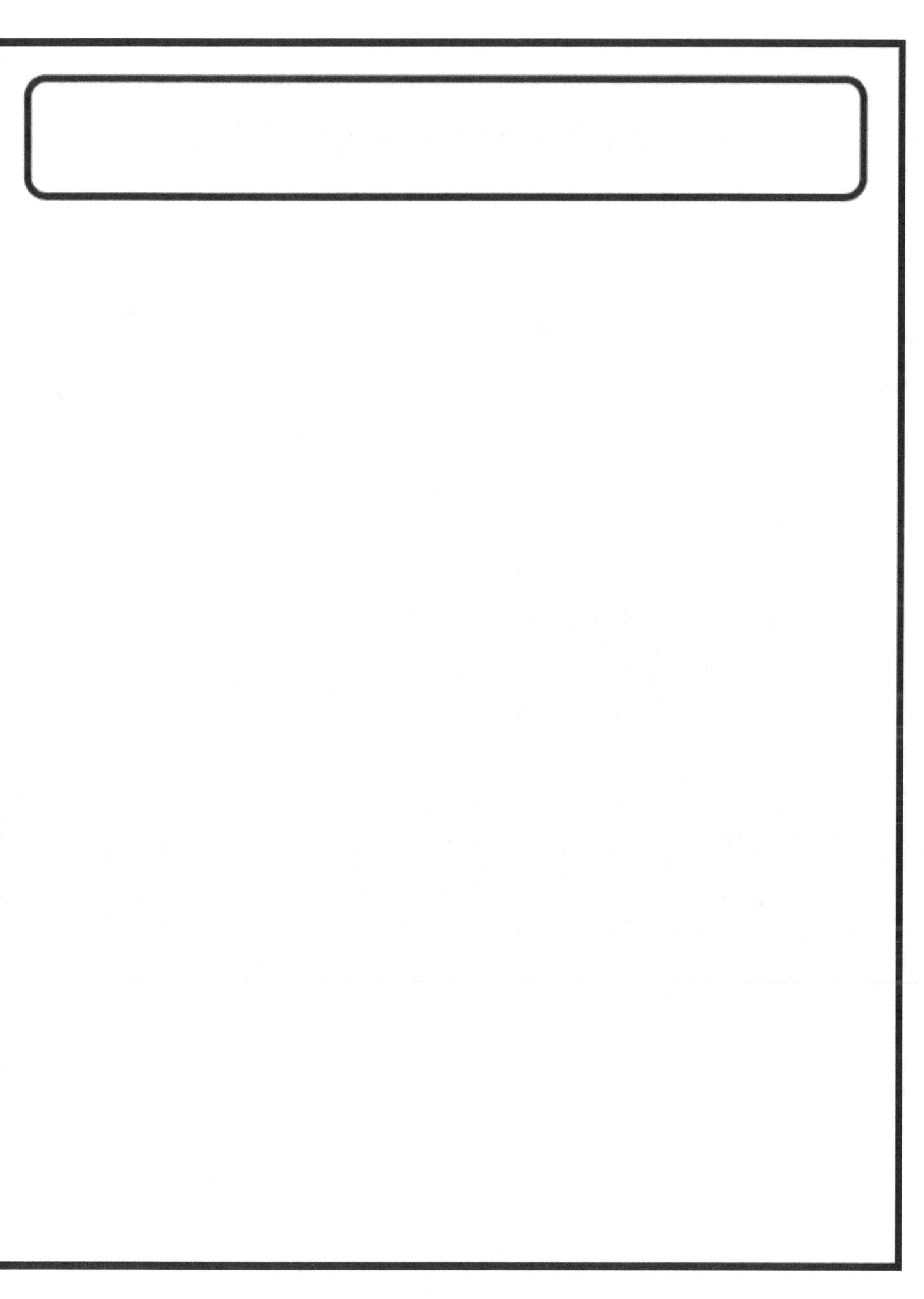

SKYSCRAPERS MALBUCH

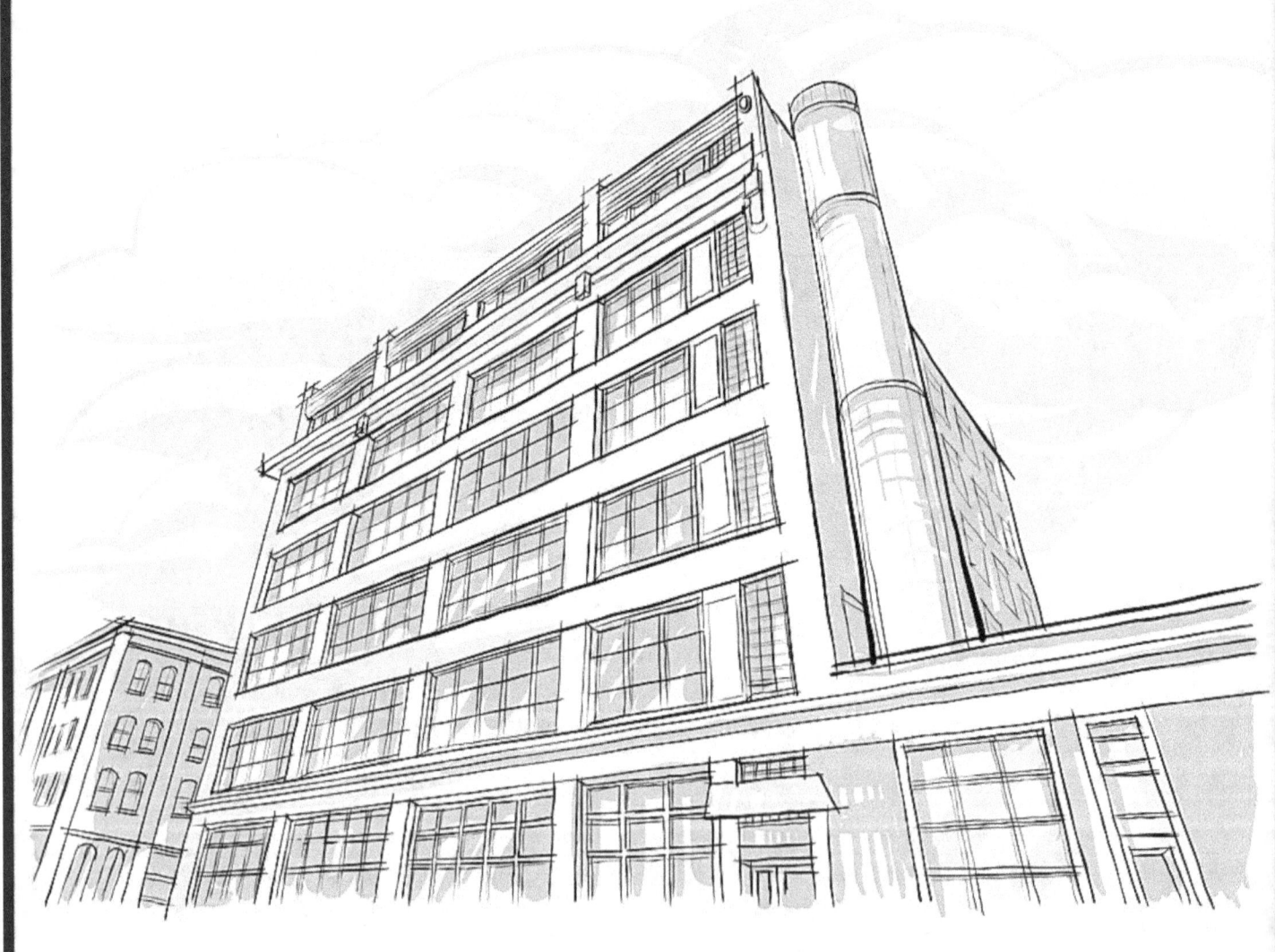

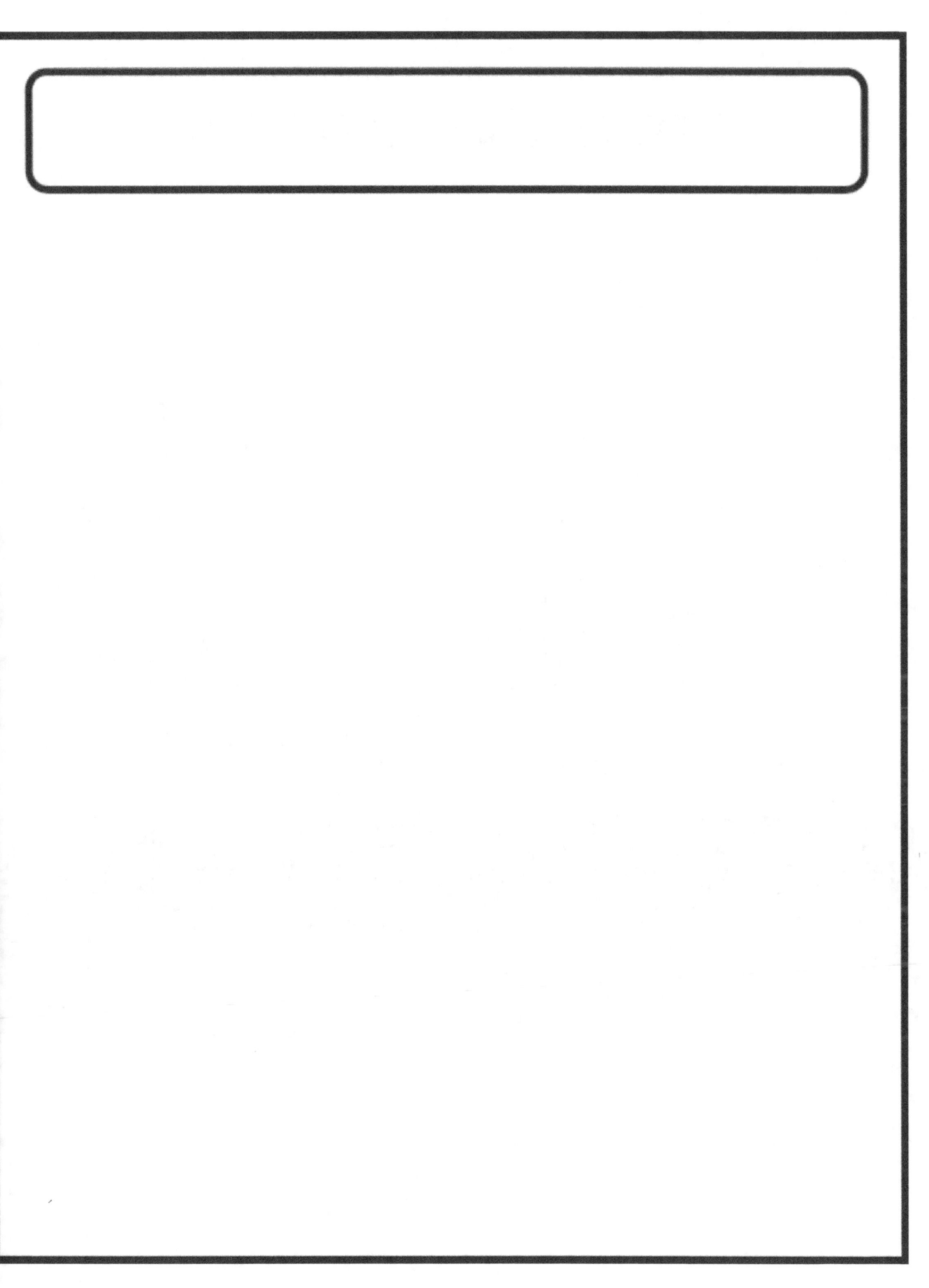

SKYSCRAPERS MALBUCH

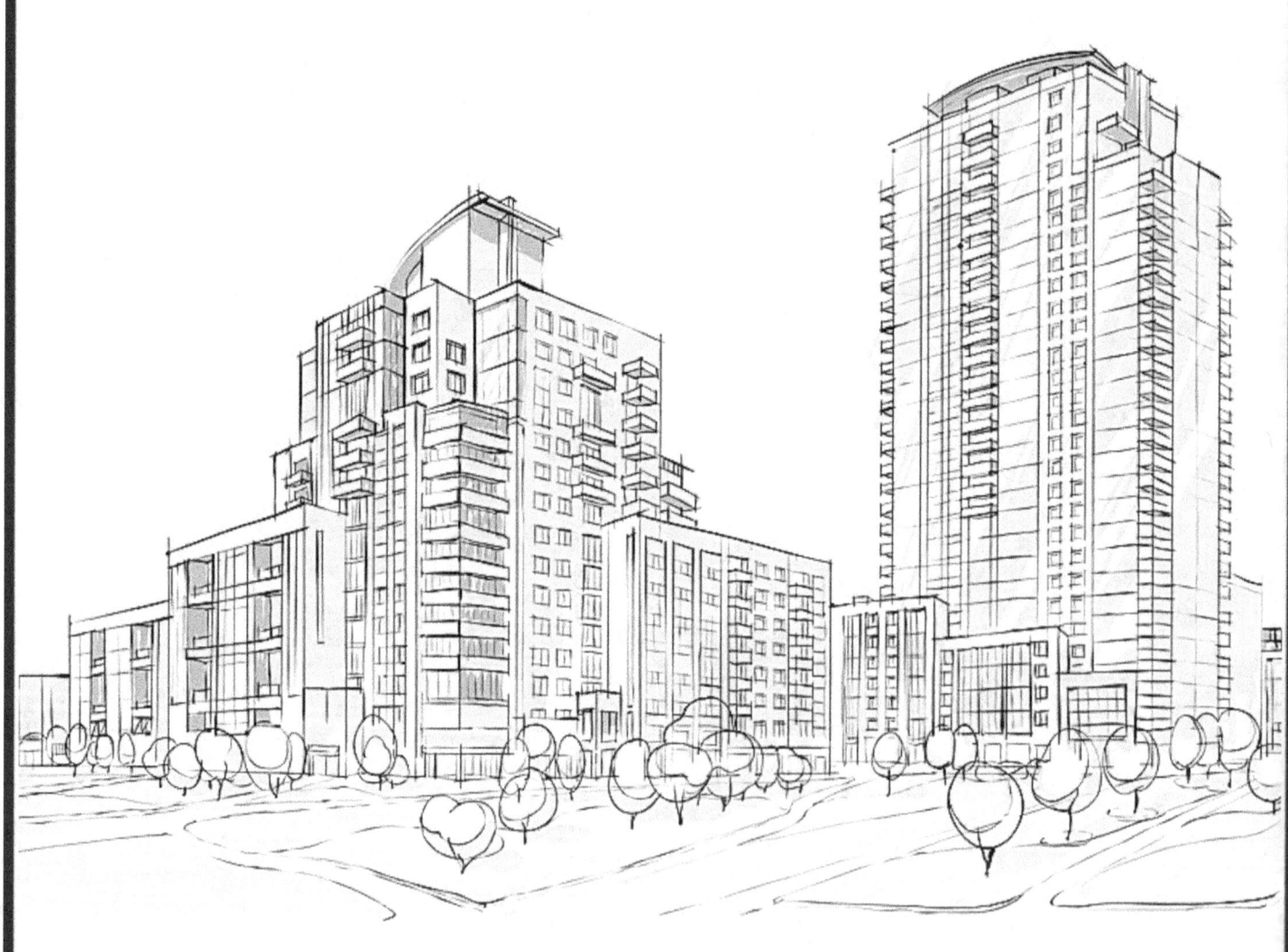

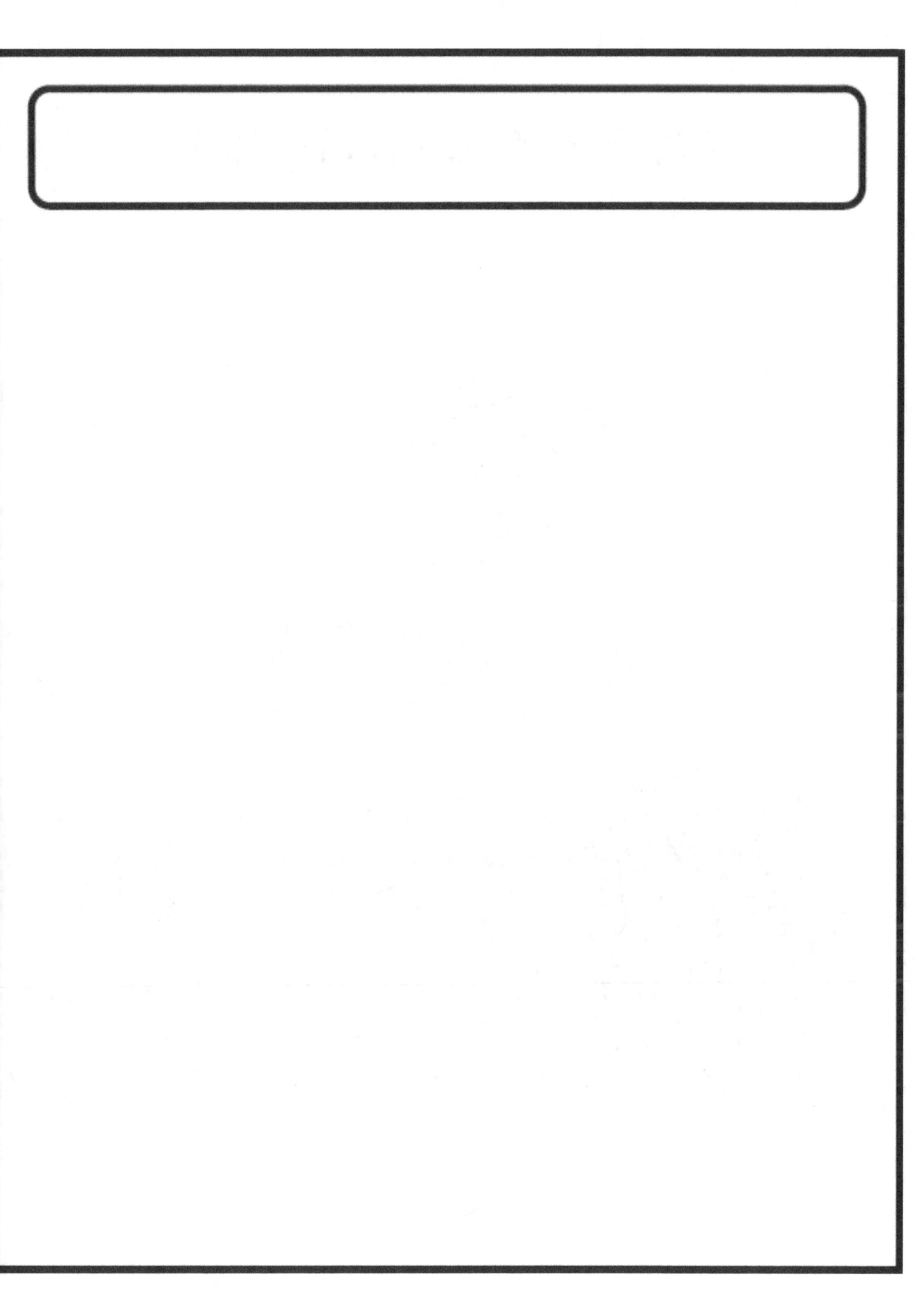

SKYSCRAPERS MALBUCH

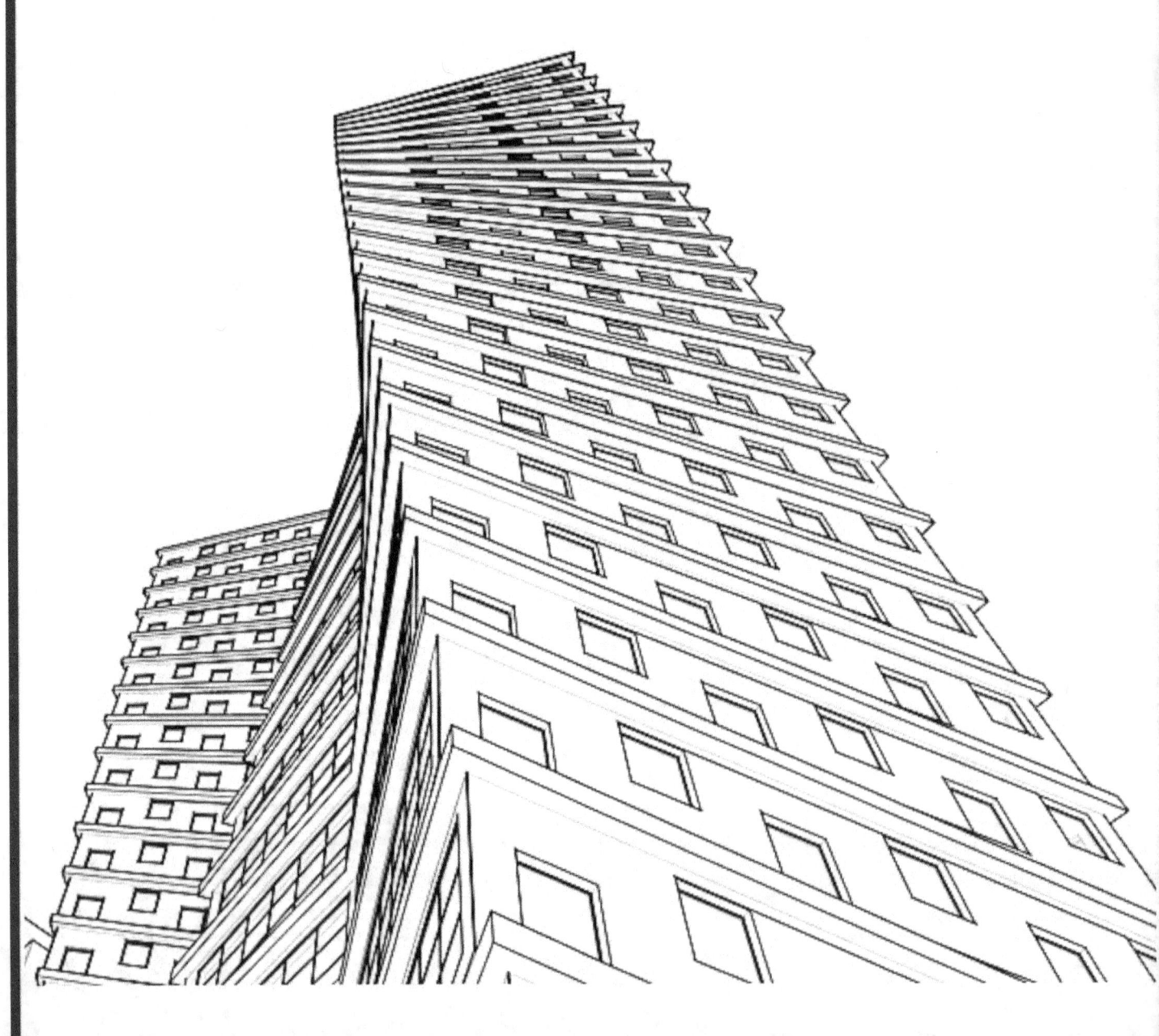

SKYSCRAPERS MALBUCH

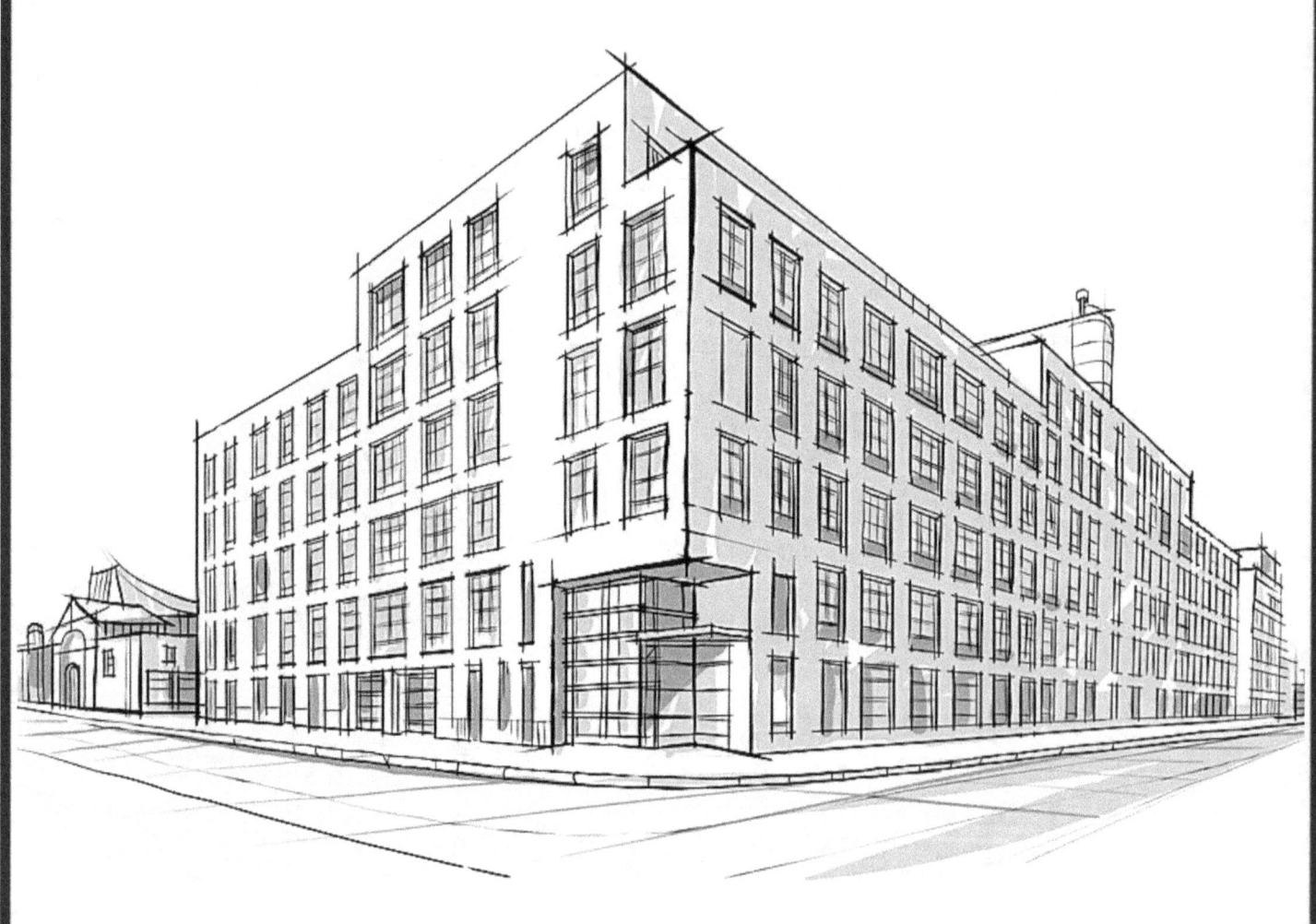

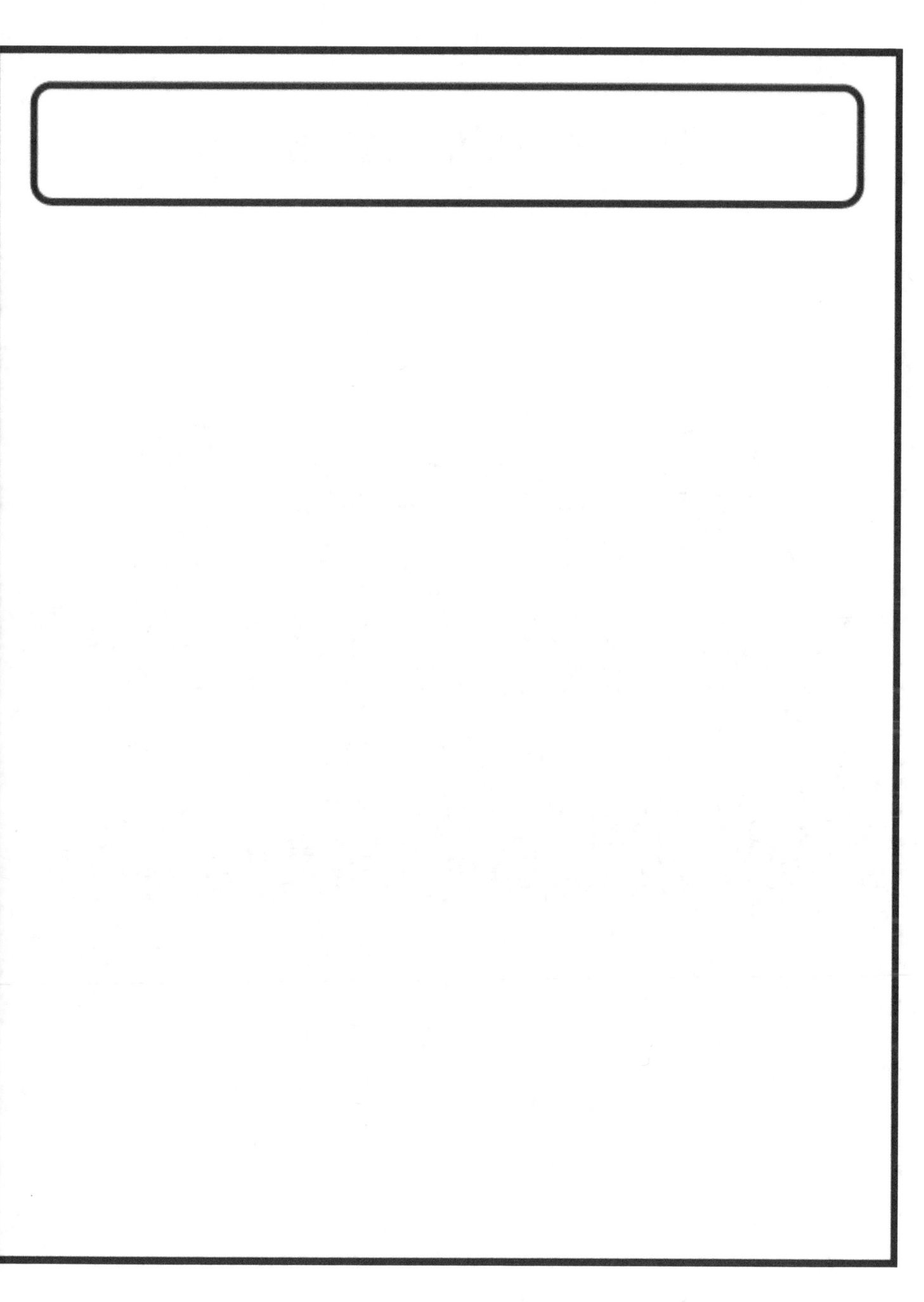

SKYSCRAPERS MALBUCH

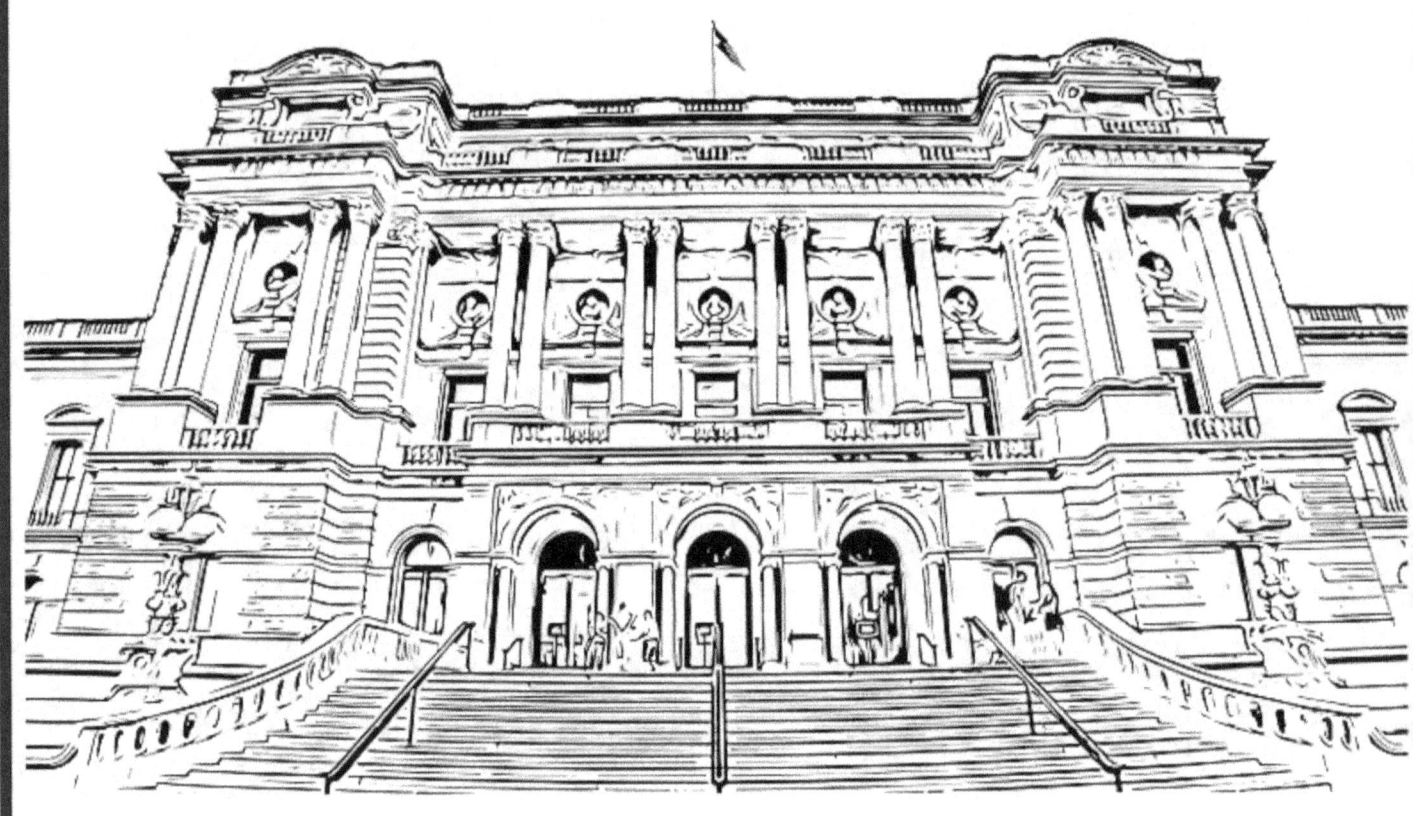

SKYSCRAPERS MALBUCH

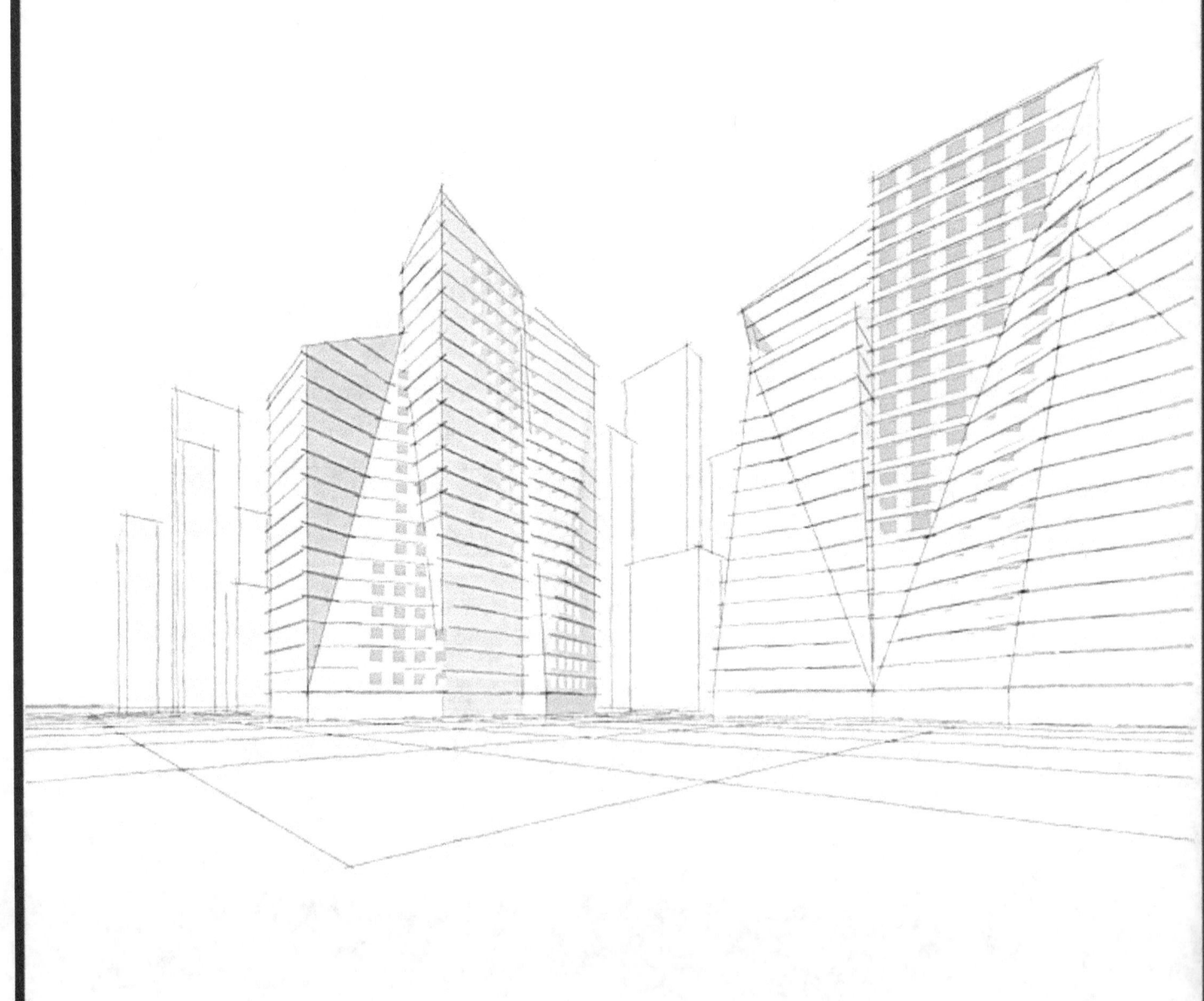

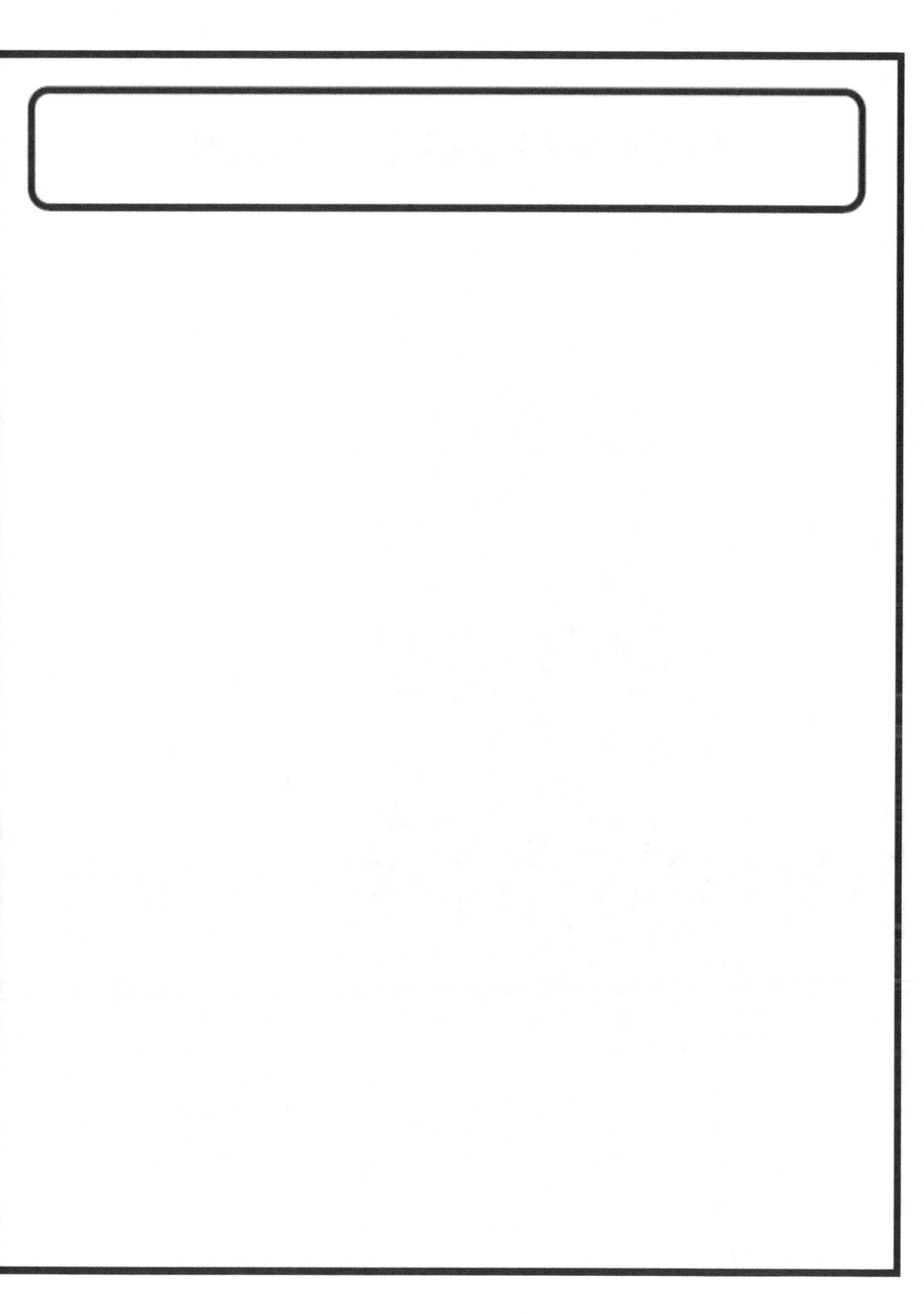

SKYSCRAPERS MALBUCH

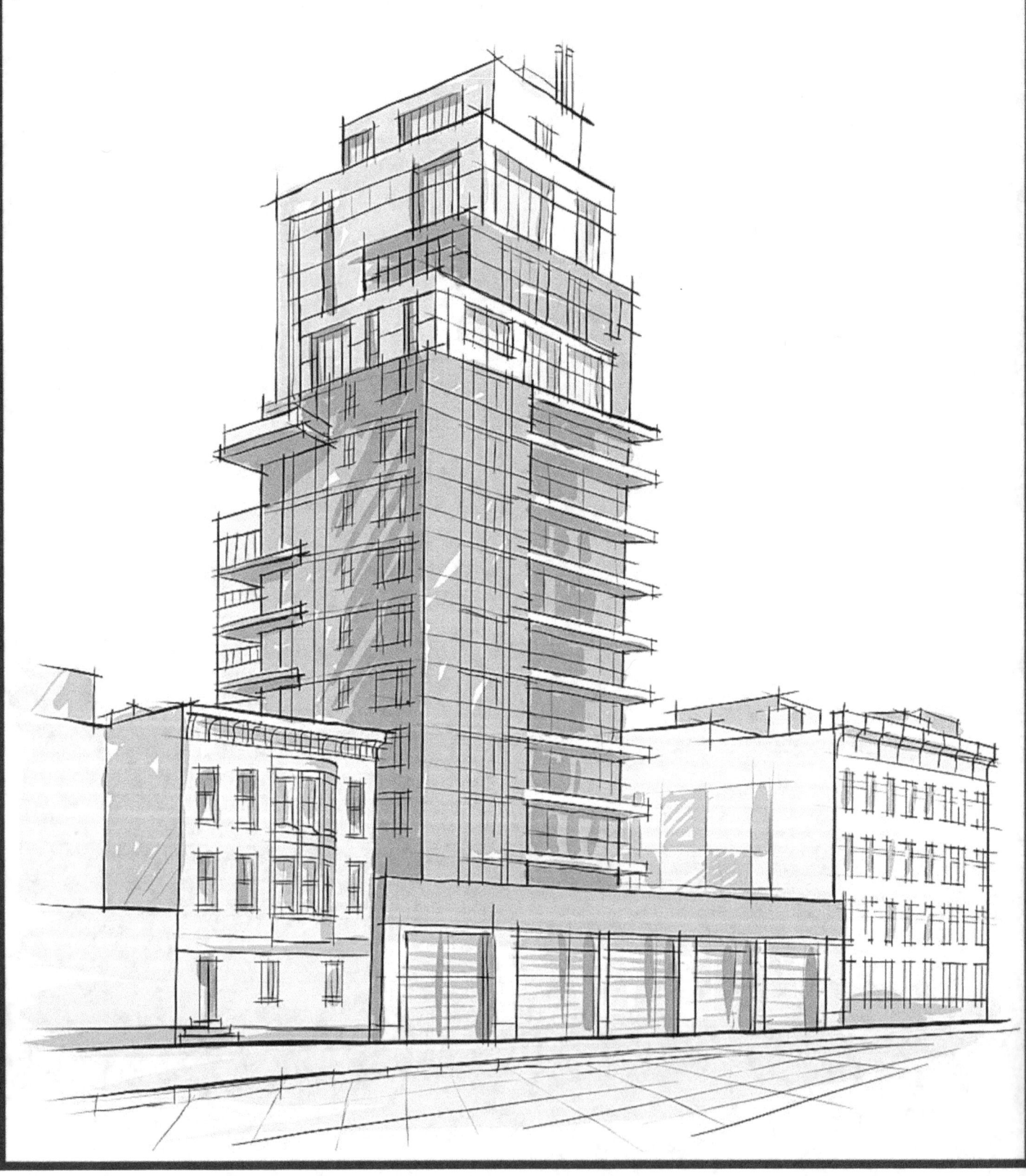

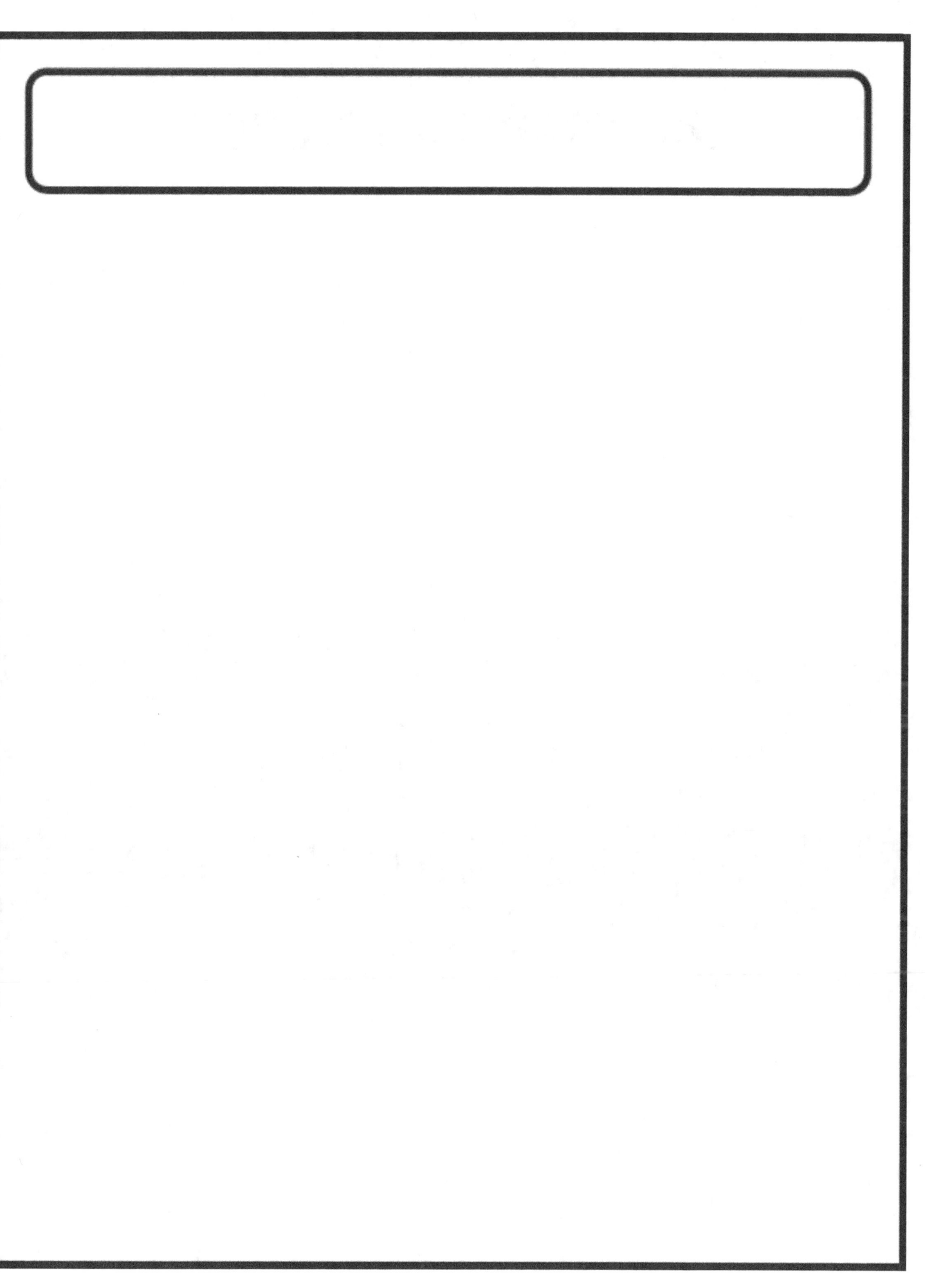

SKYSCRAPERS MALBUCH

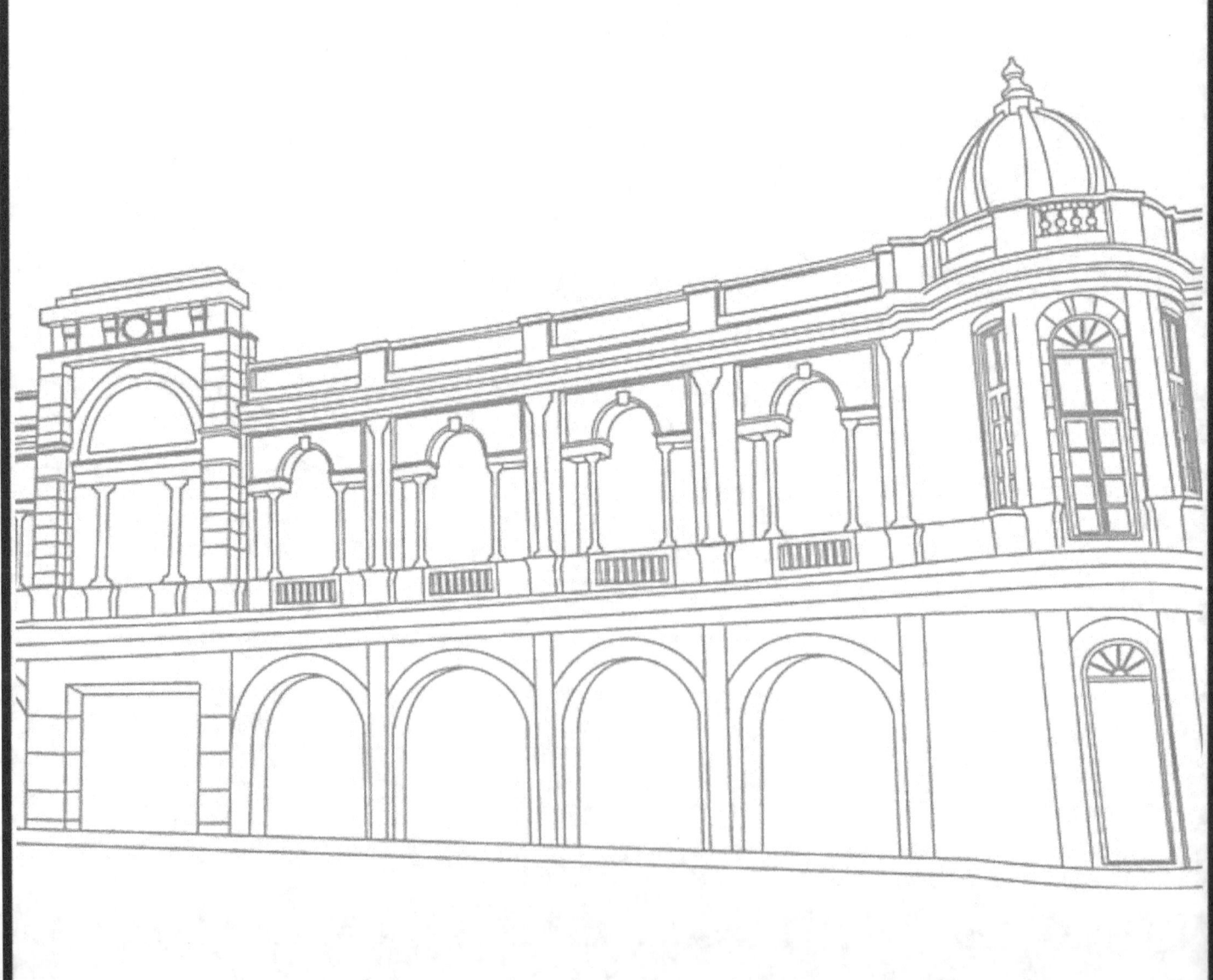

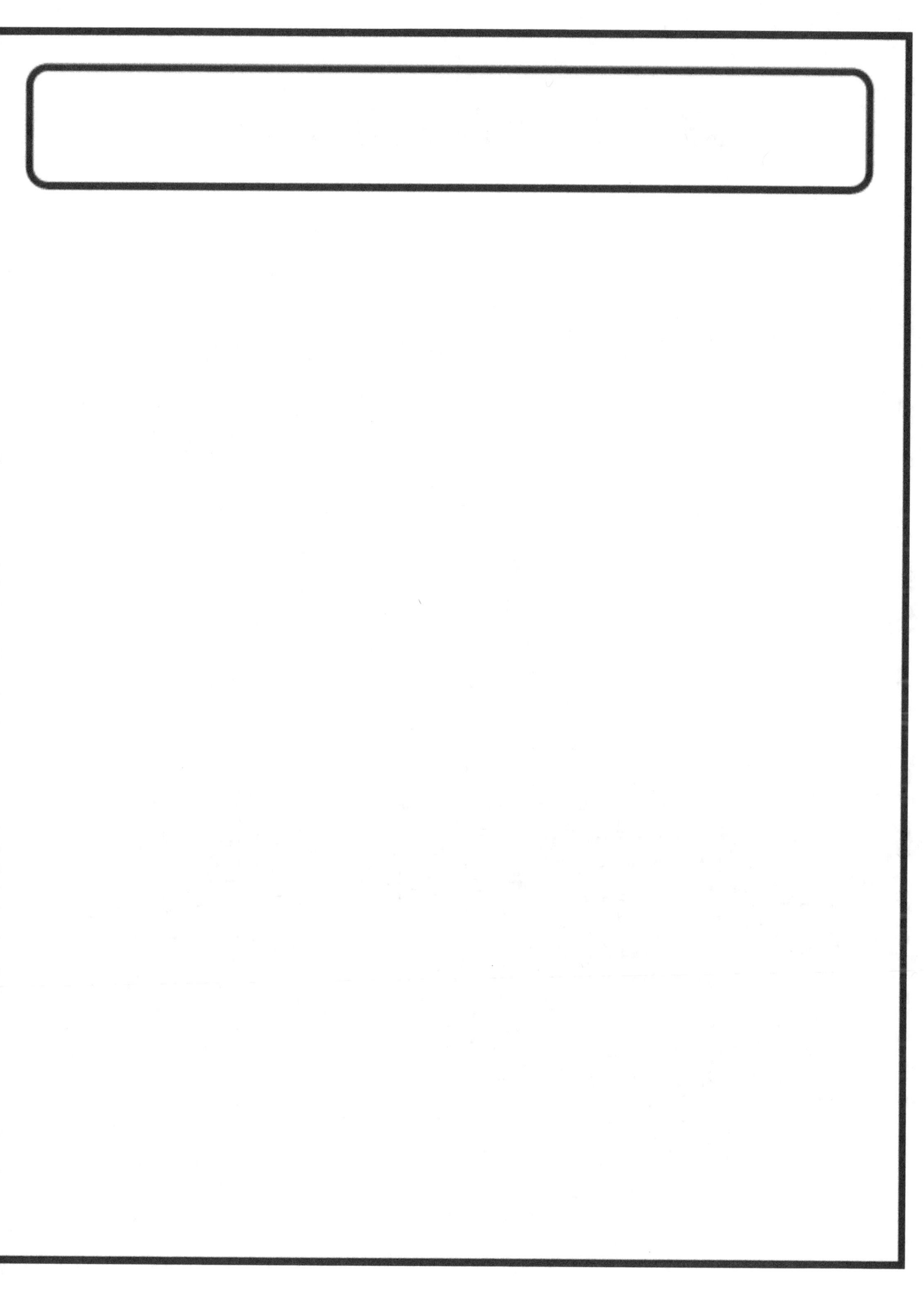

SKYSCRAPERS MALBUCH

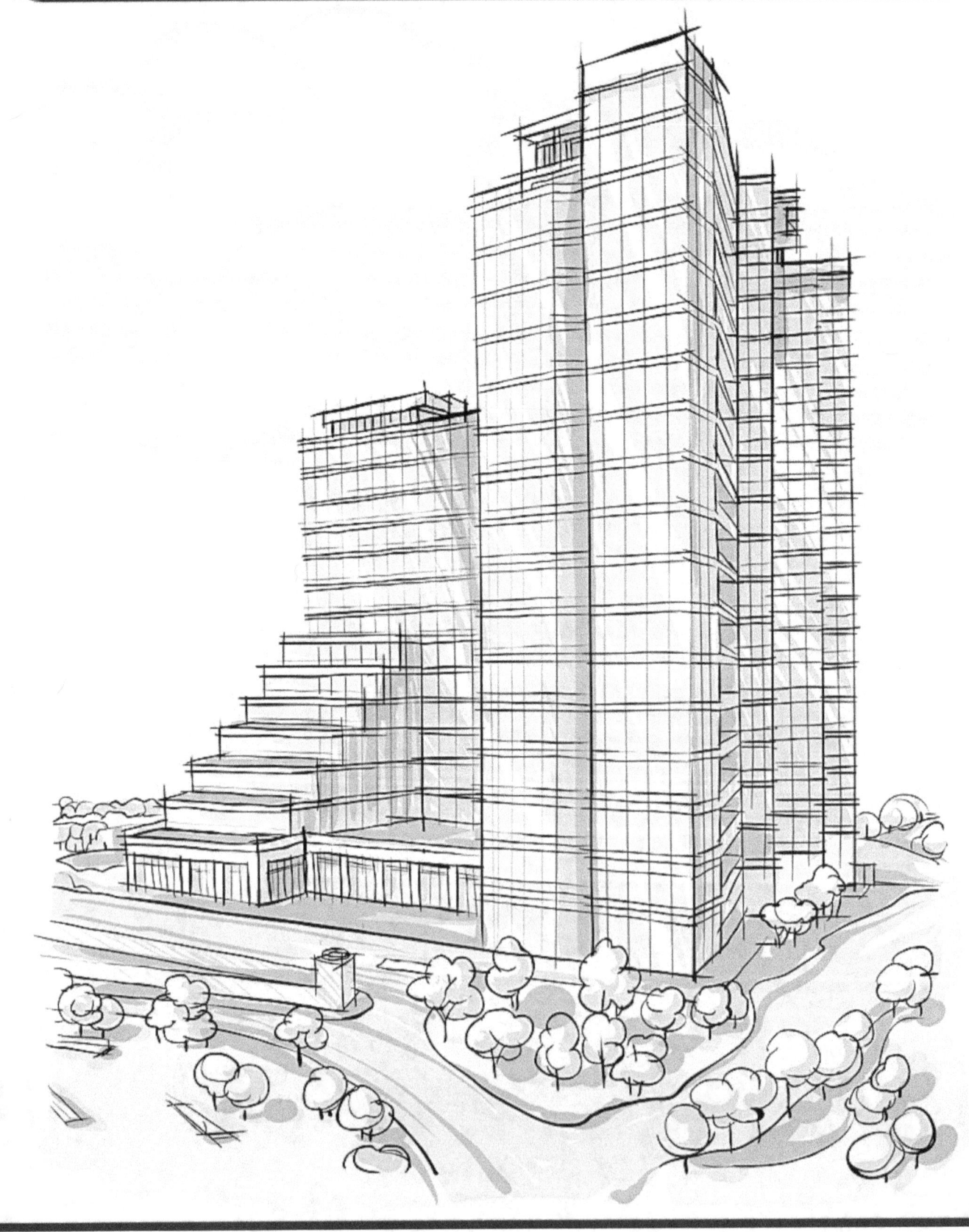

SKYSCRAPERS MALBUCH

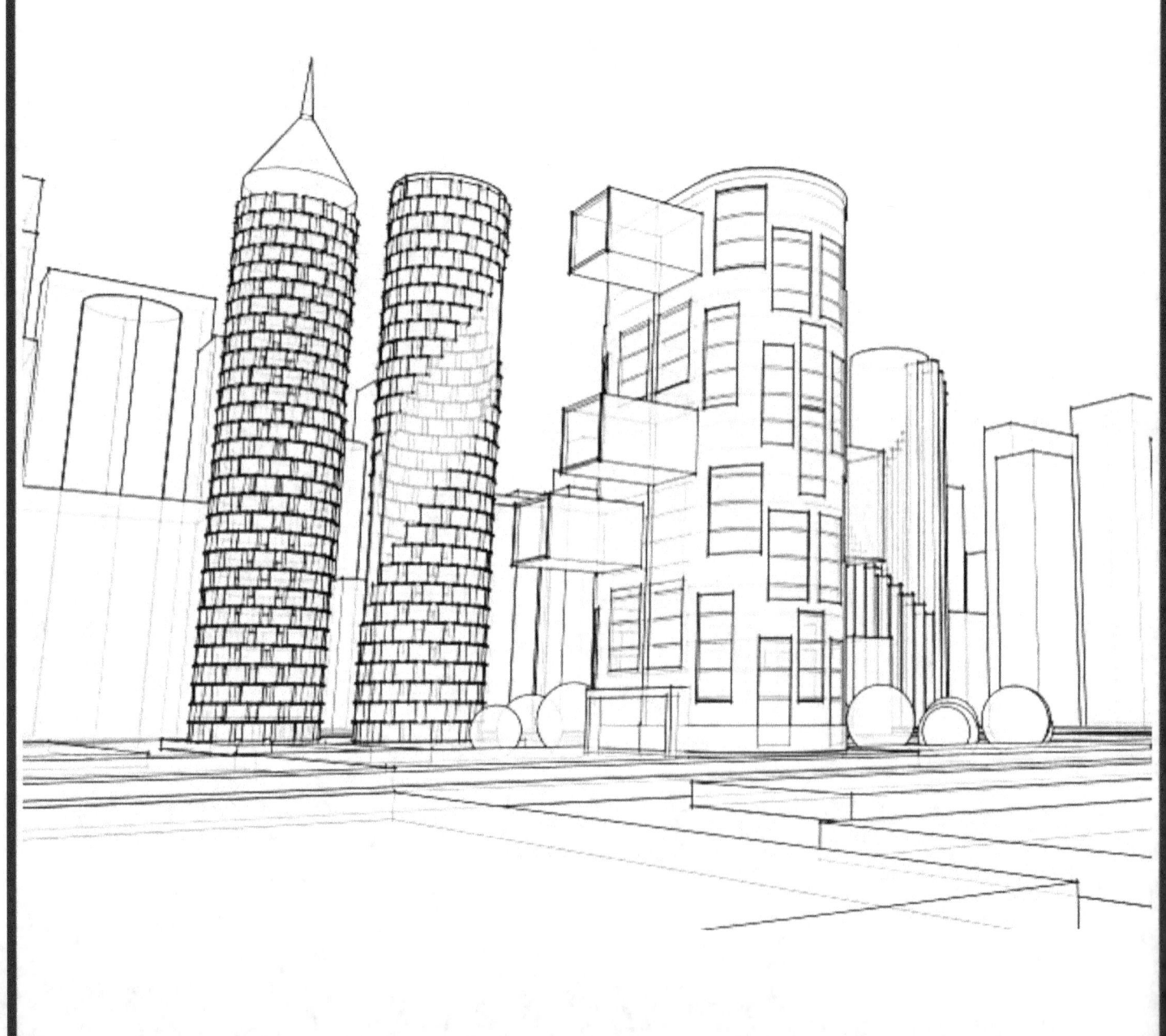

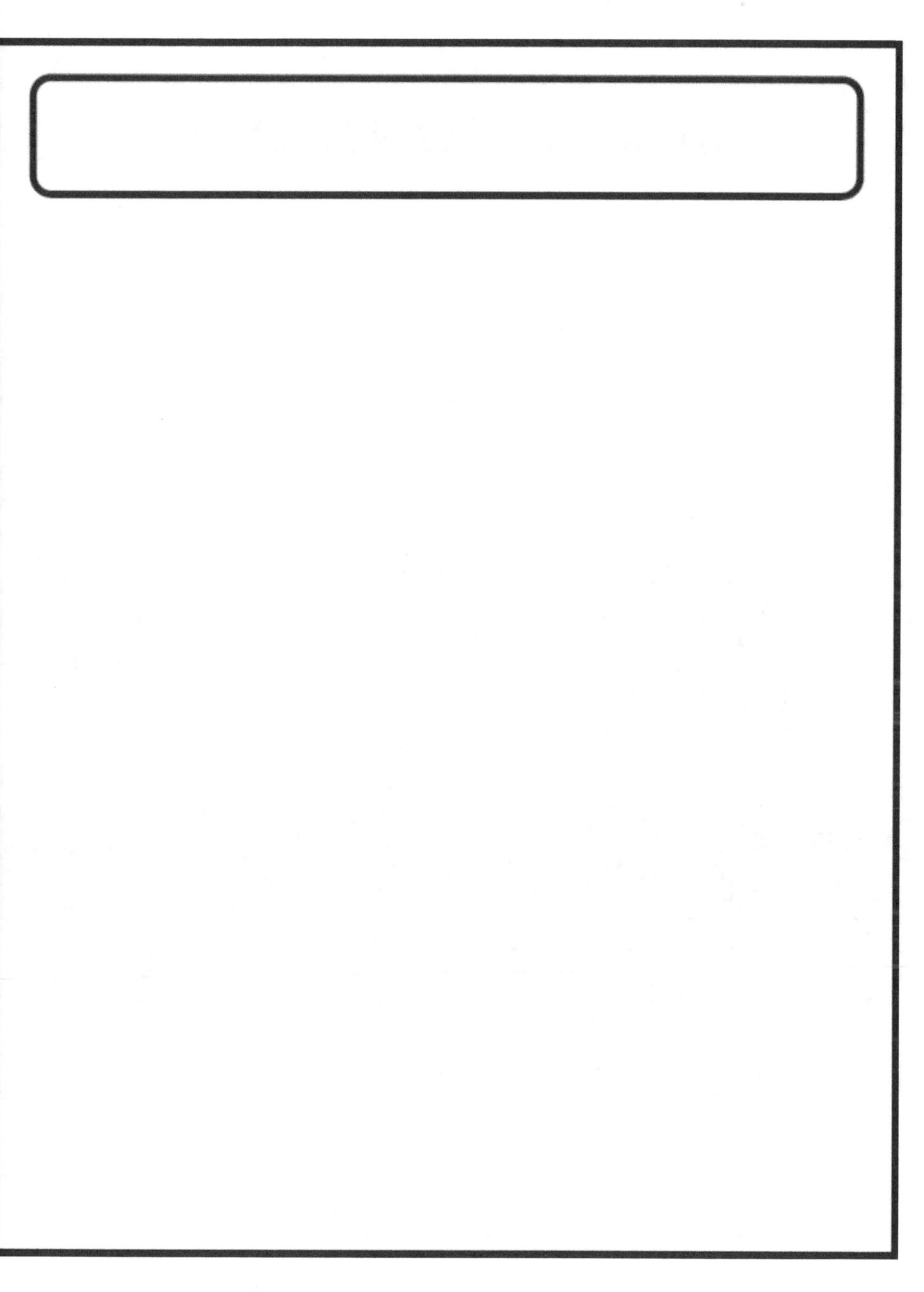

SKYSCRAPERS MALBUCH

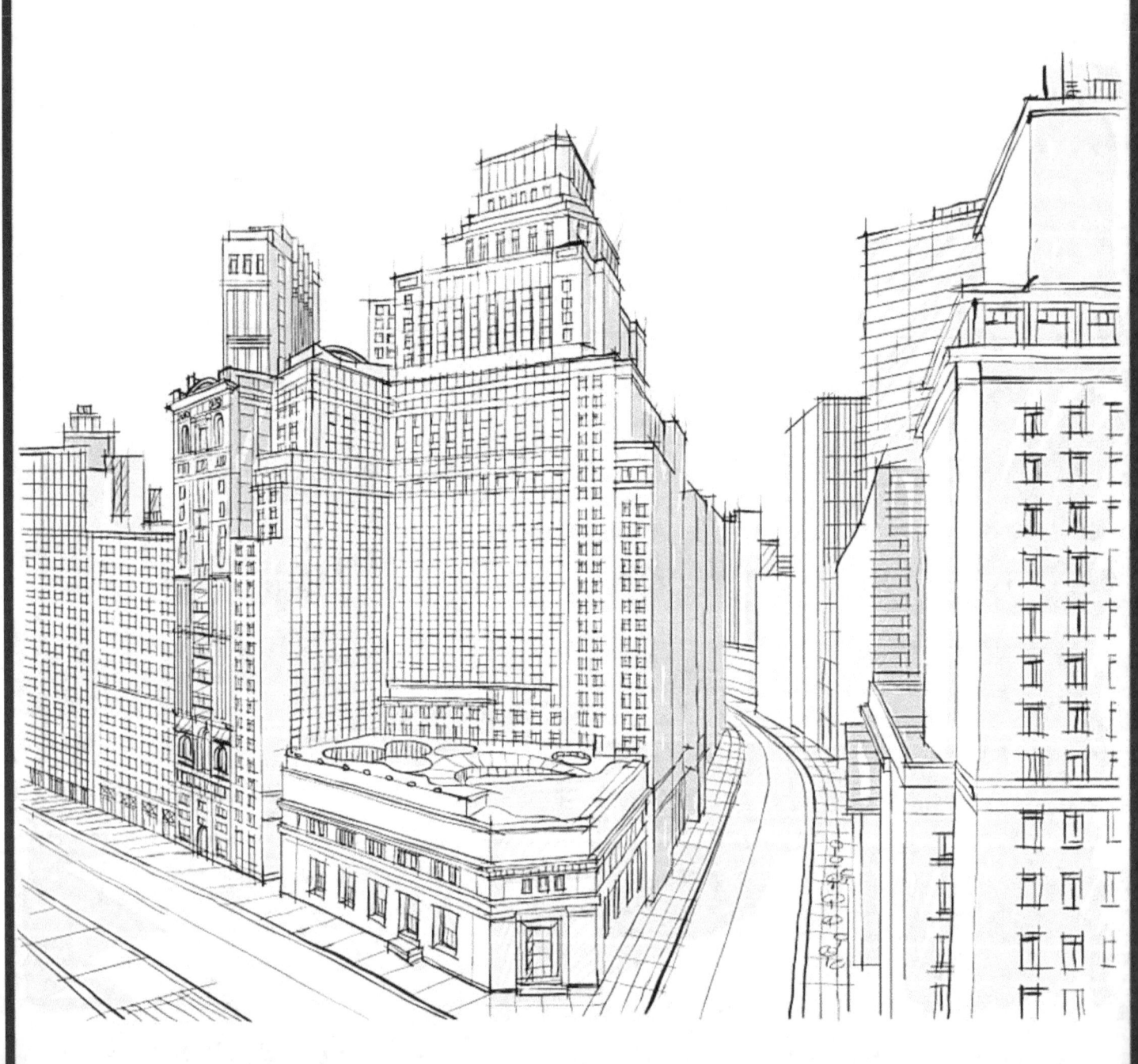

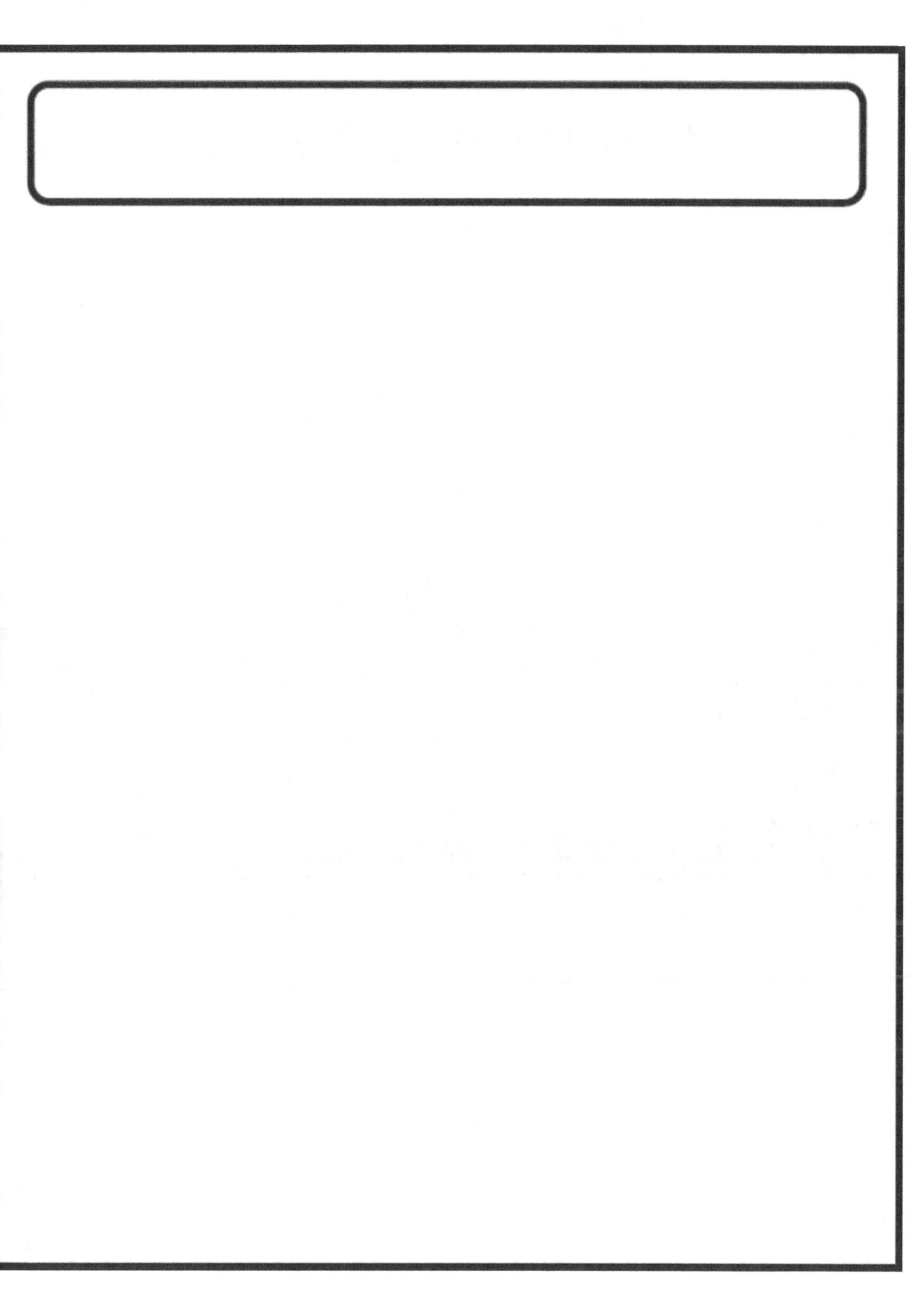

SKYSCRAPERS MALBUCH

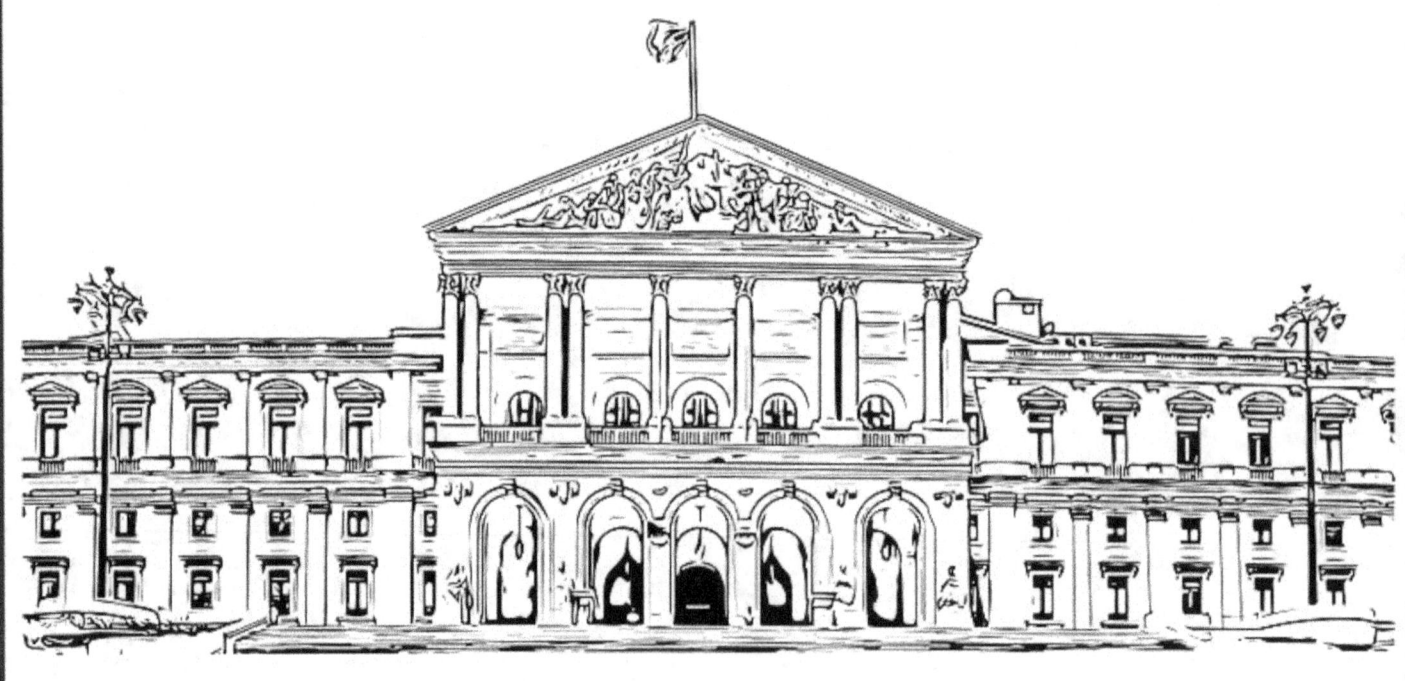

SKYSCRAPERS MALBUCH

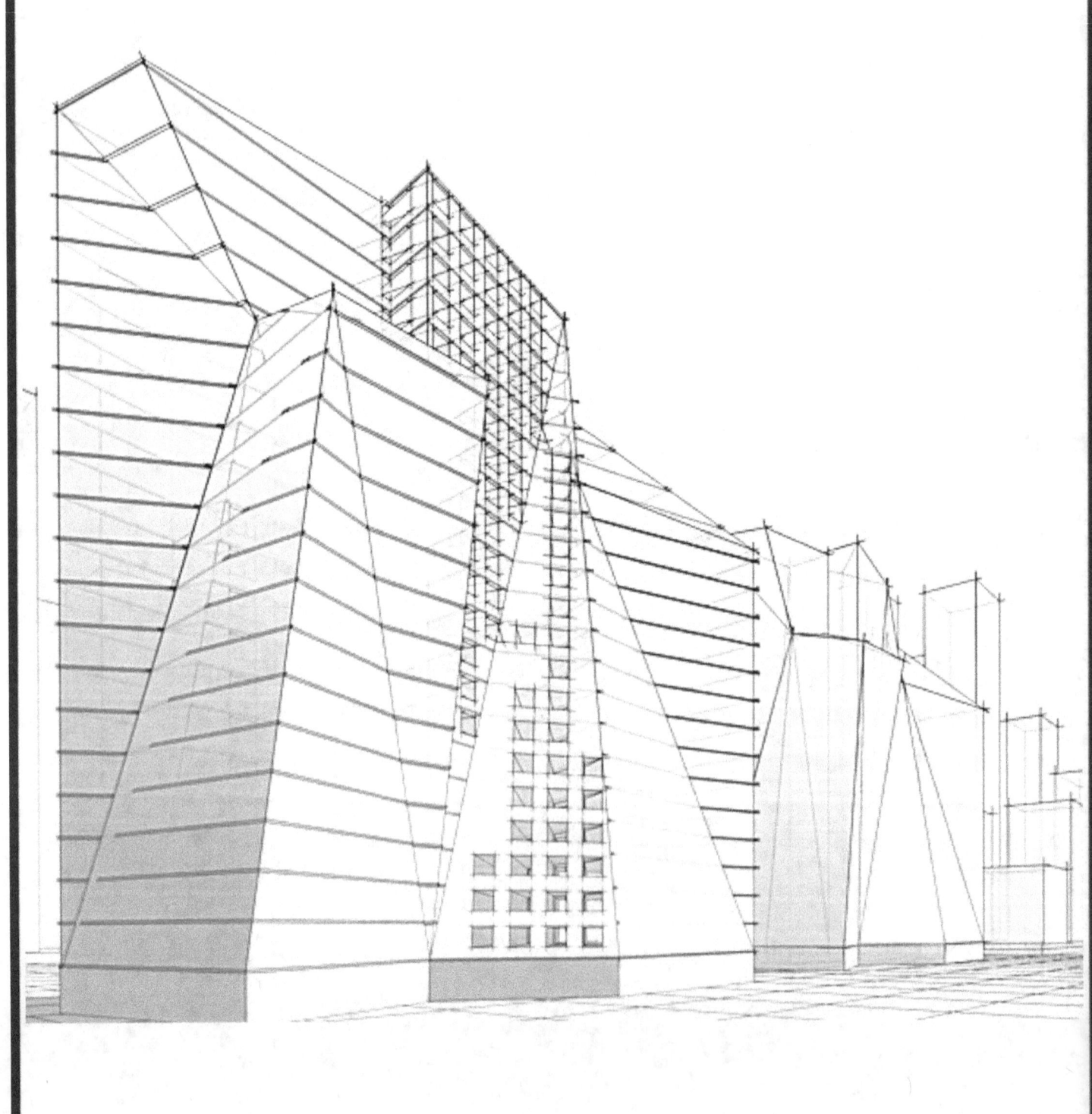

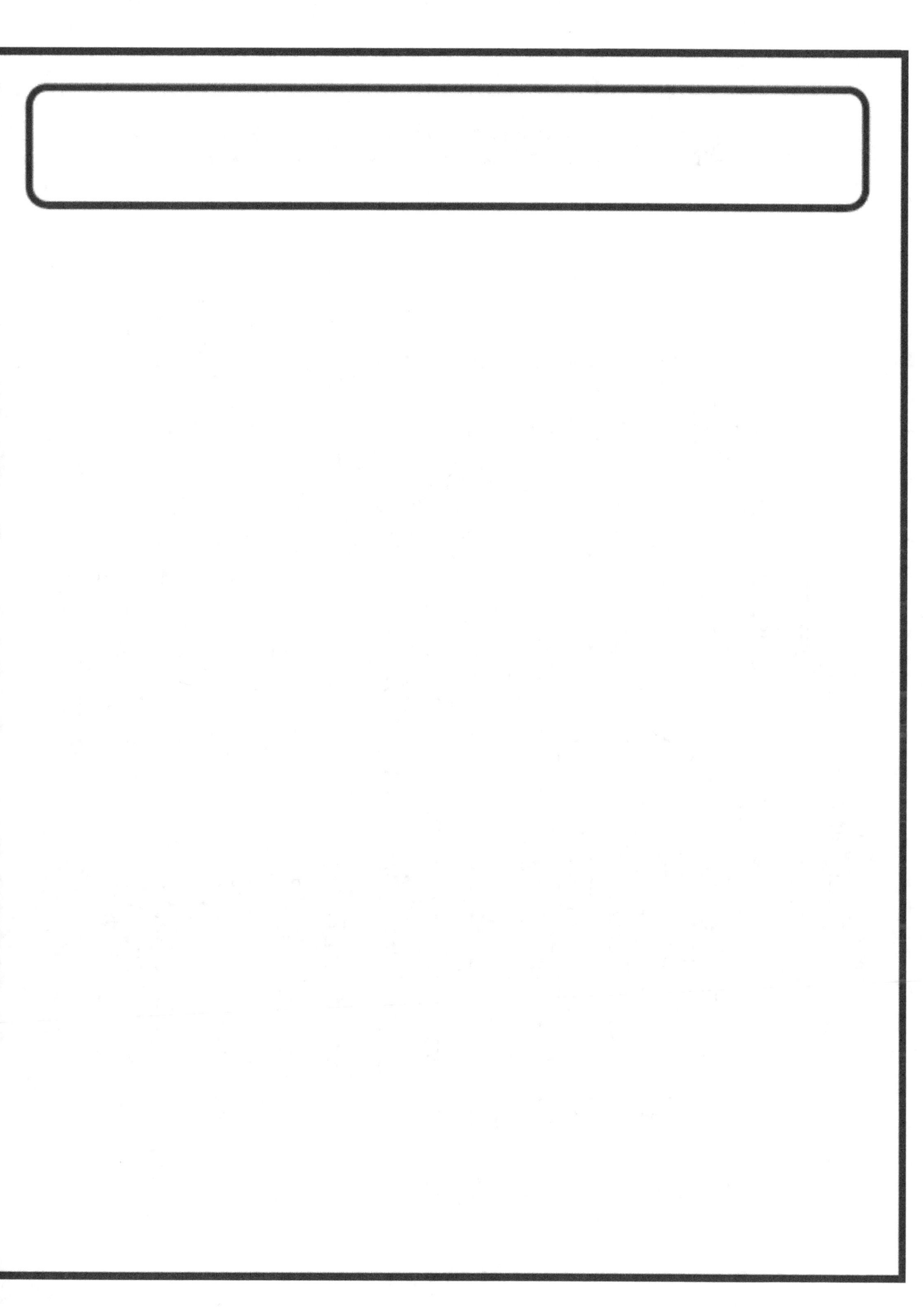

SKYSCRAPERS MALBUCH

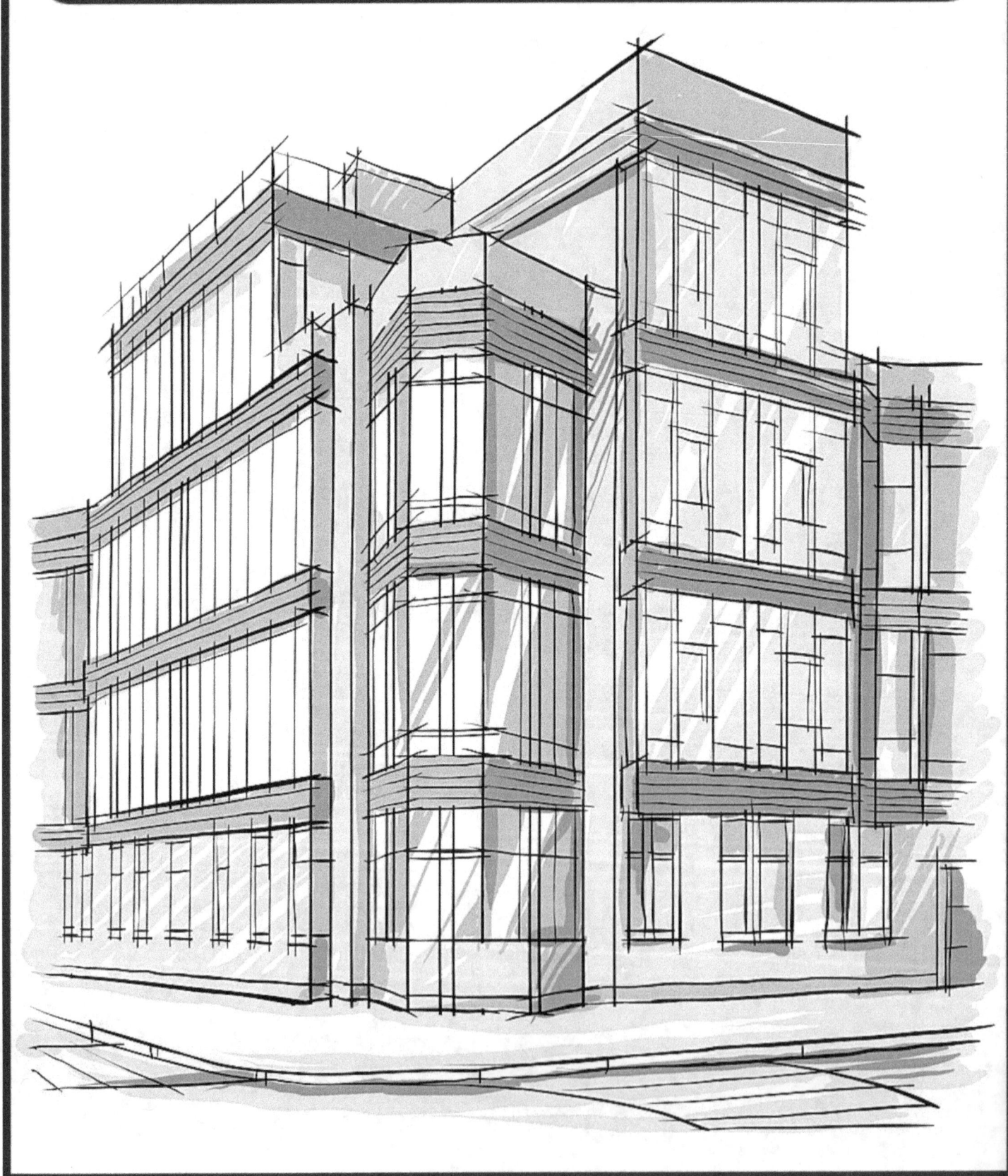

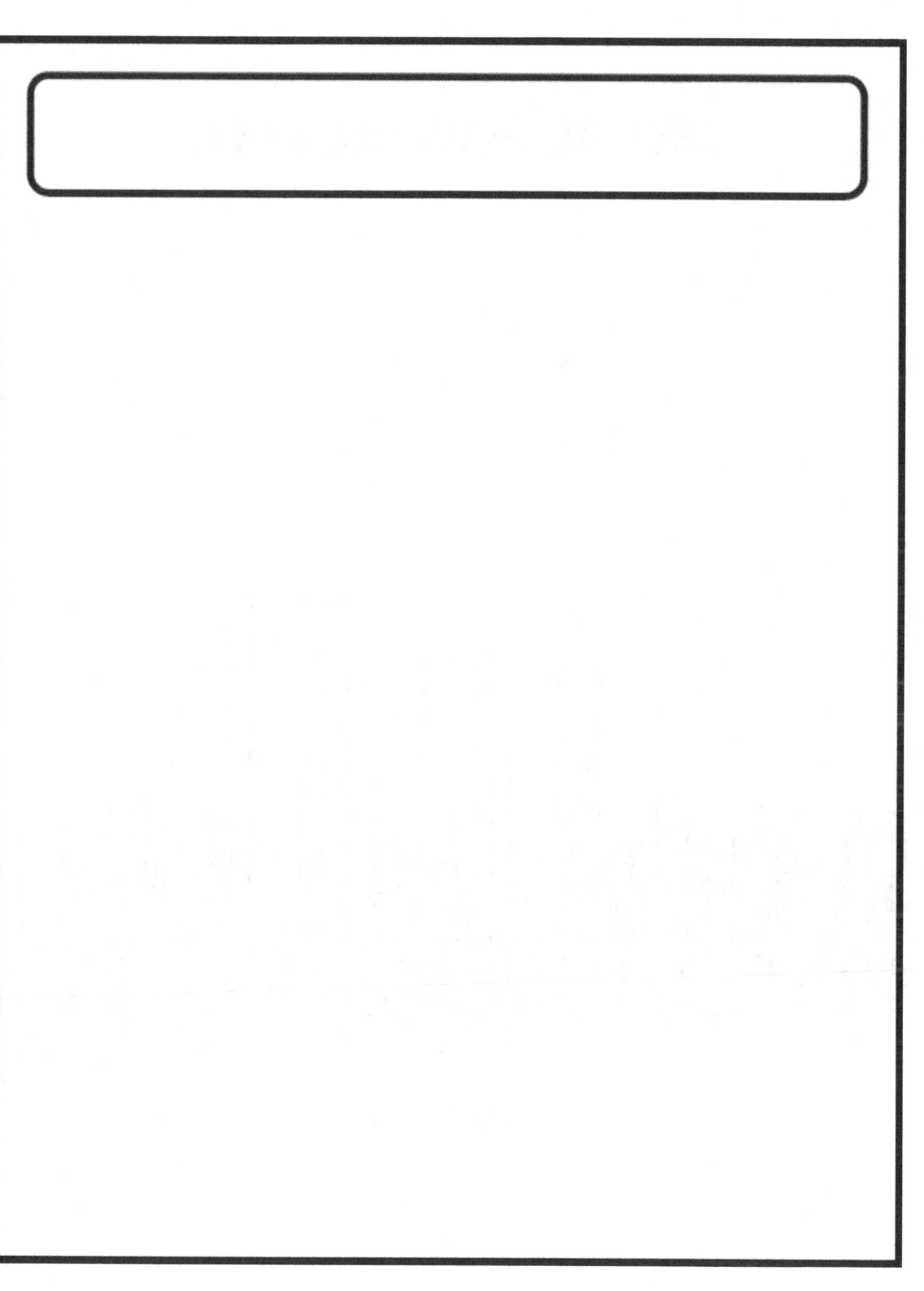

SKYSCRAPERS MALBUCH

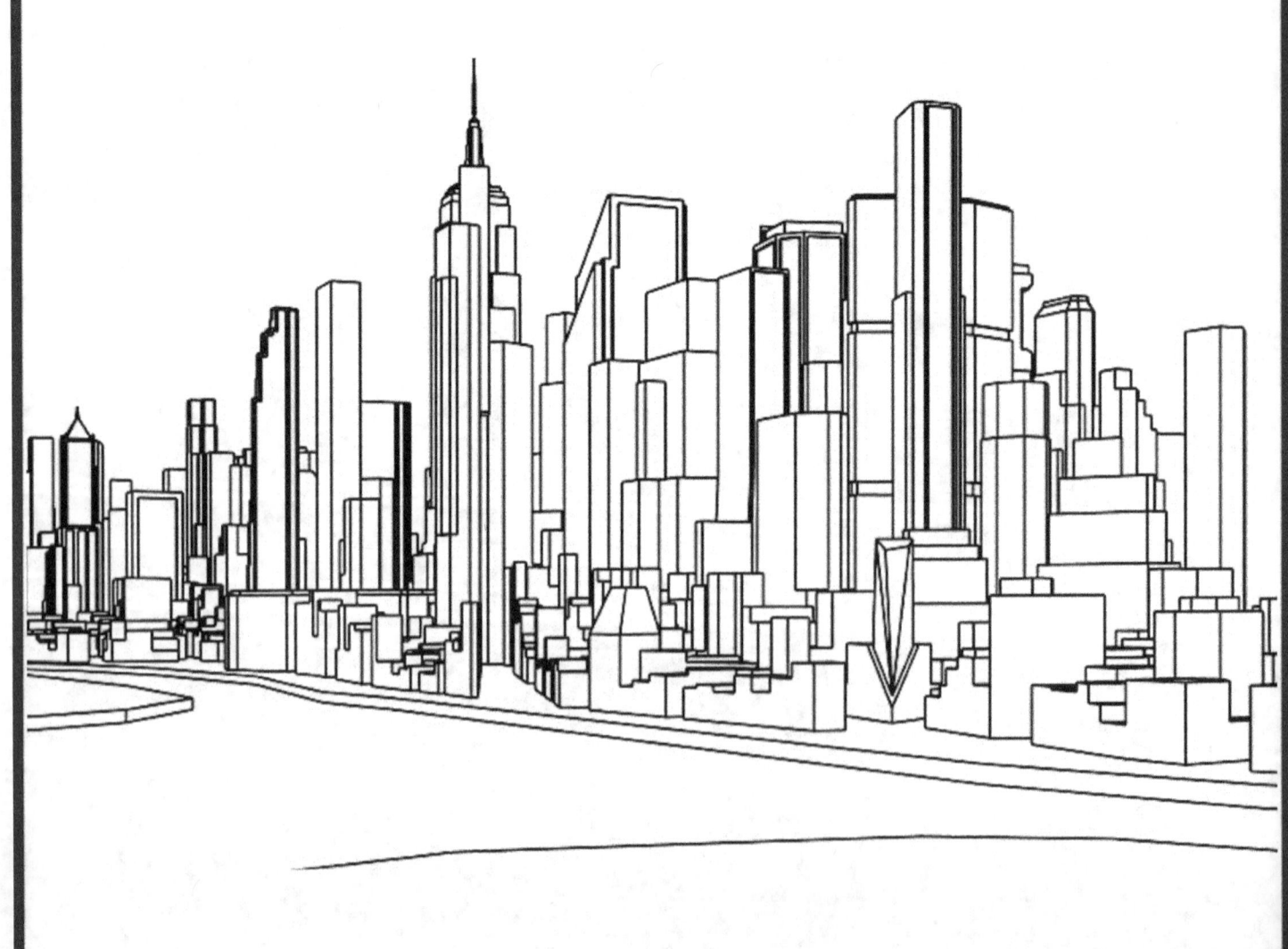

SKYSCRAPERS MALBUCH

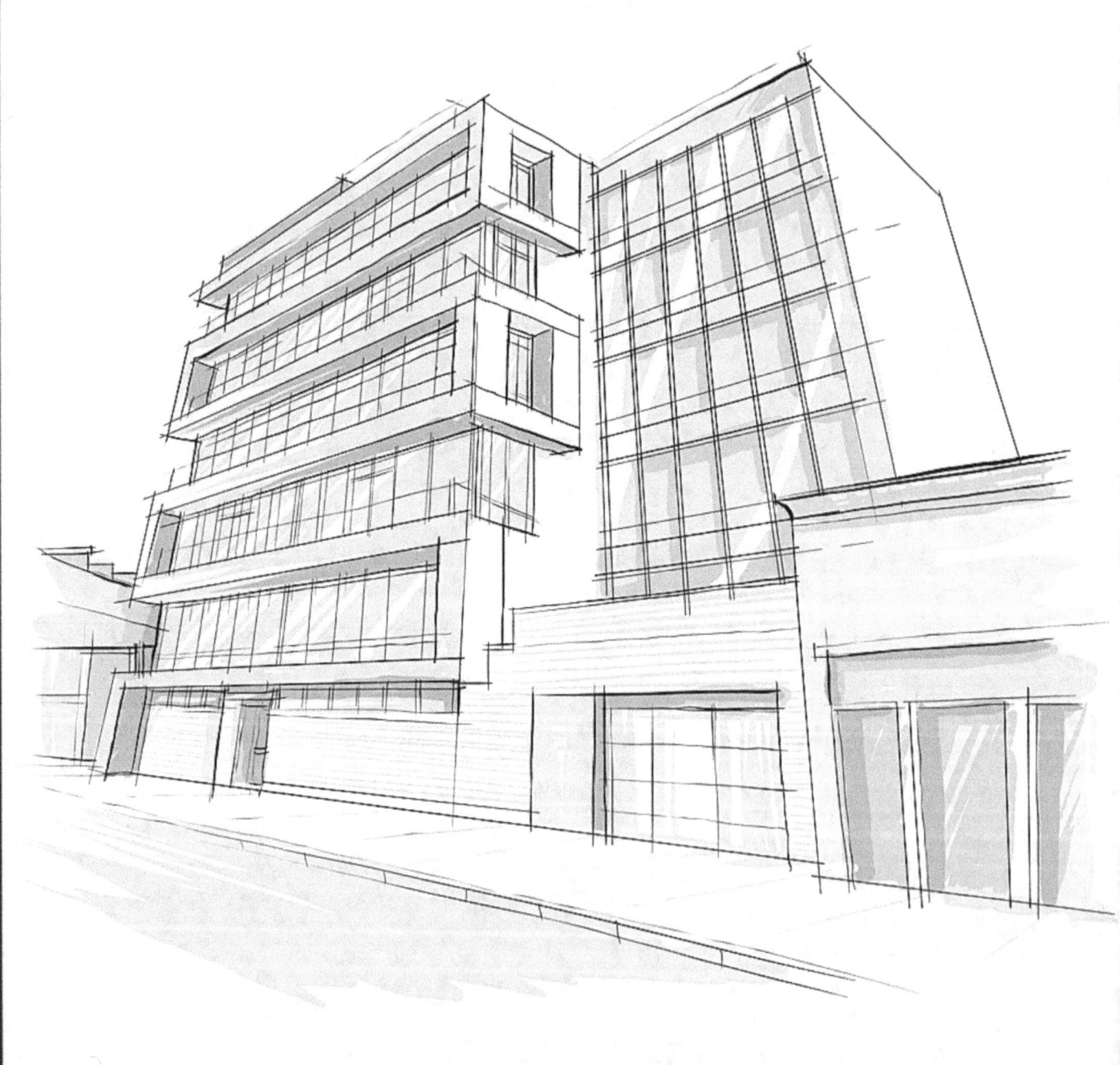

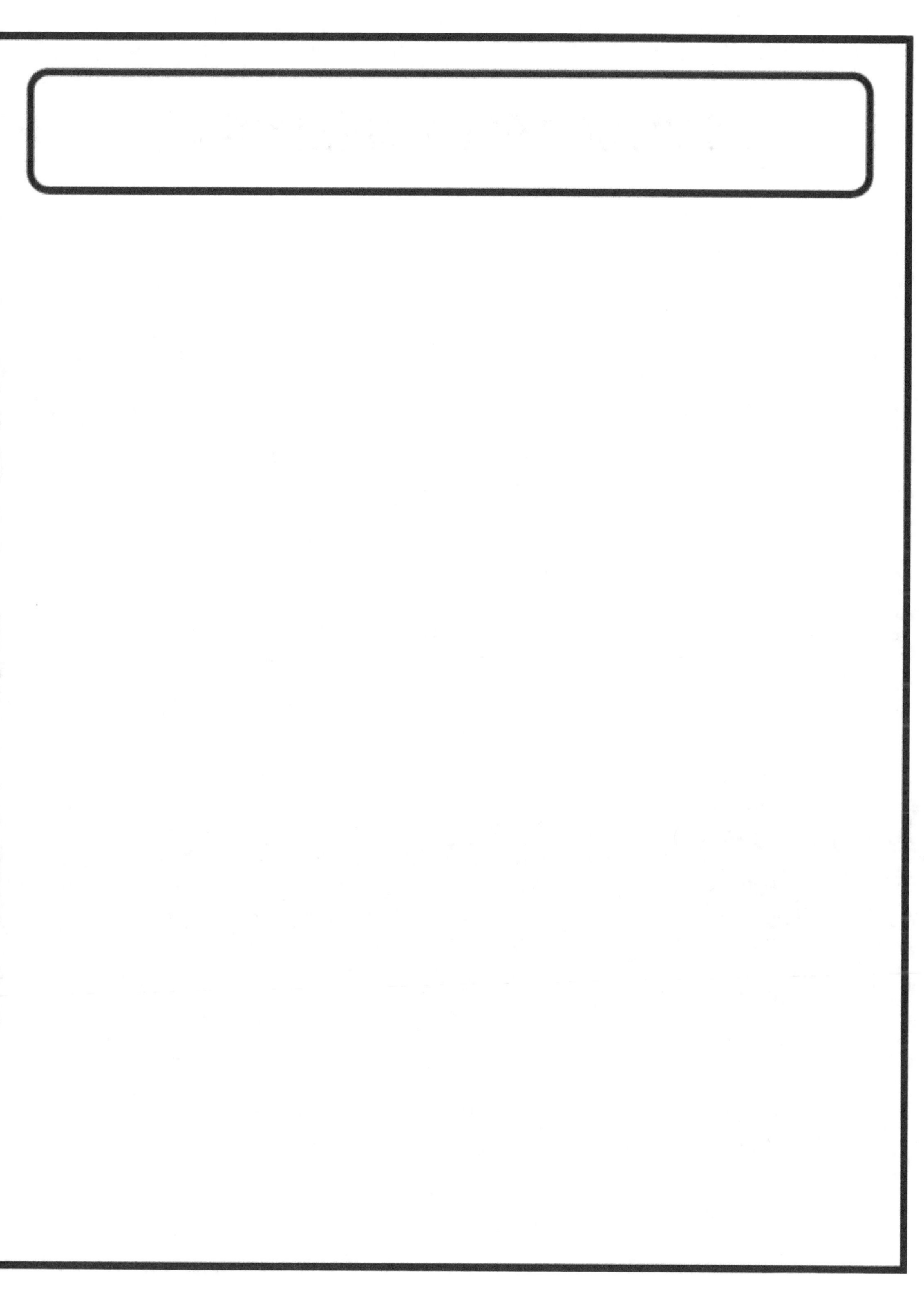

SKYSCRAPERS MALBUCH

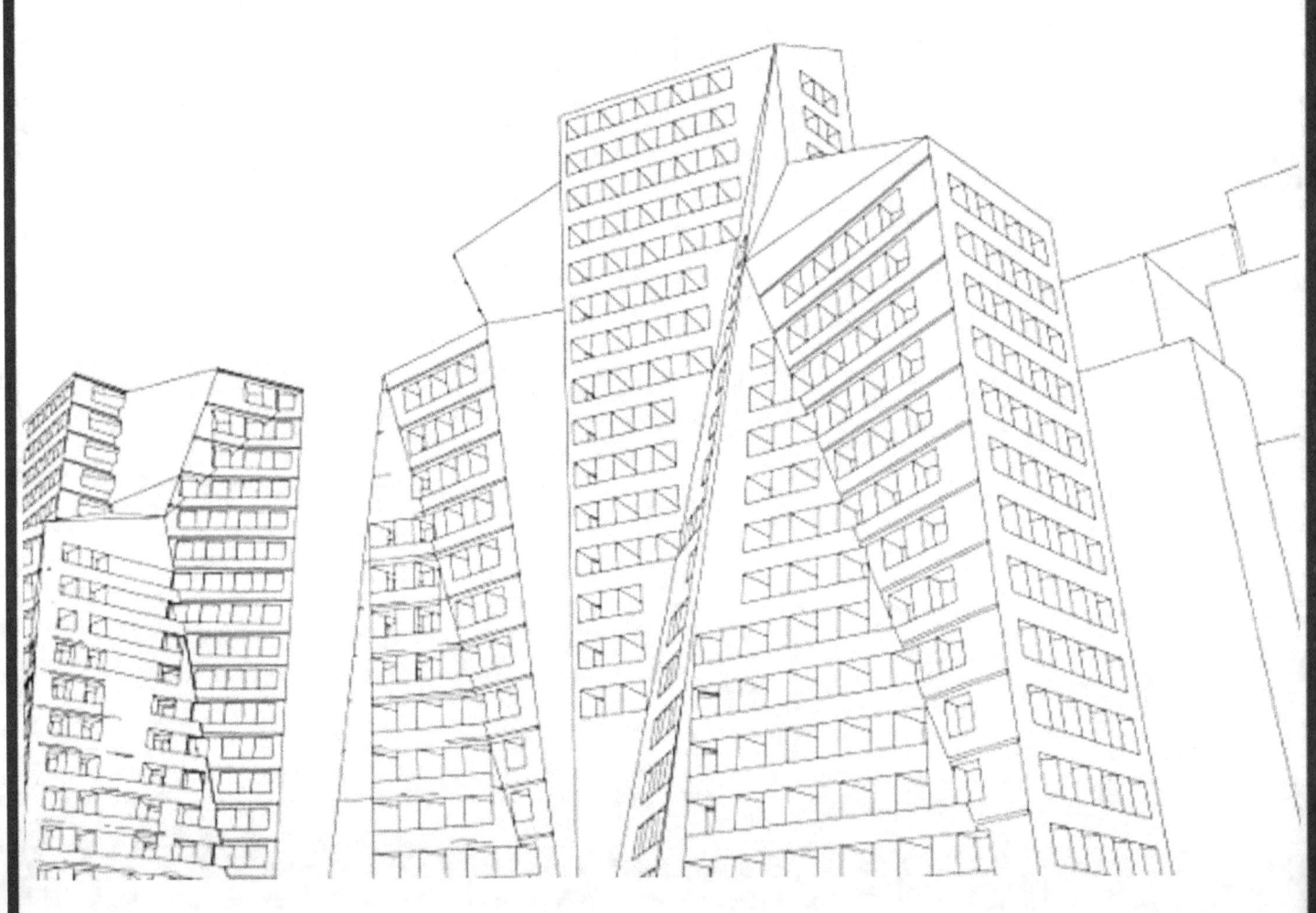

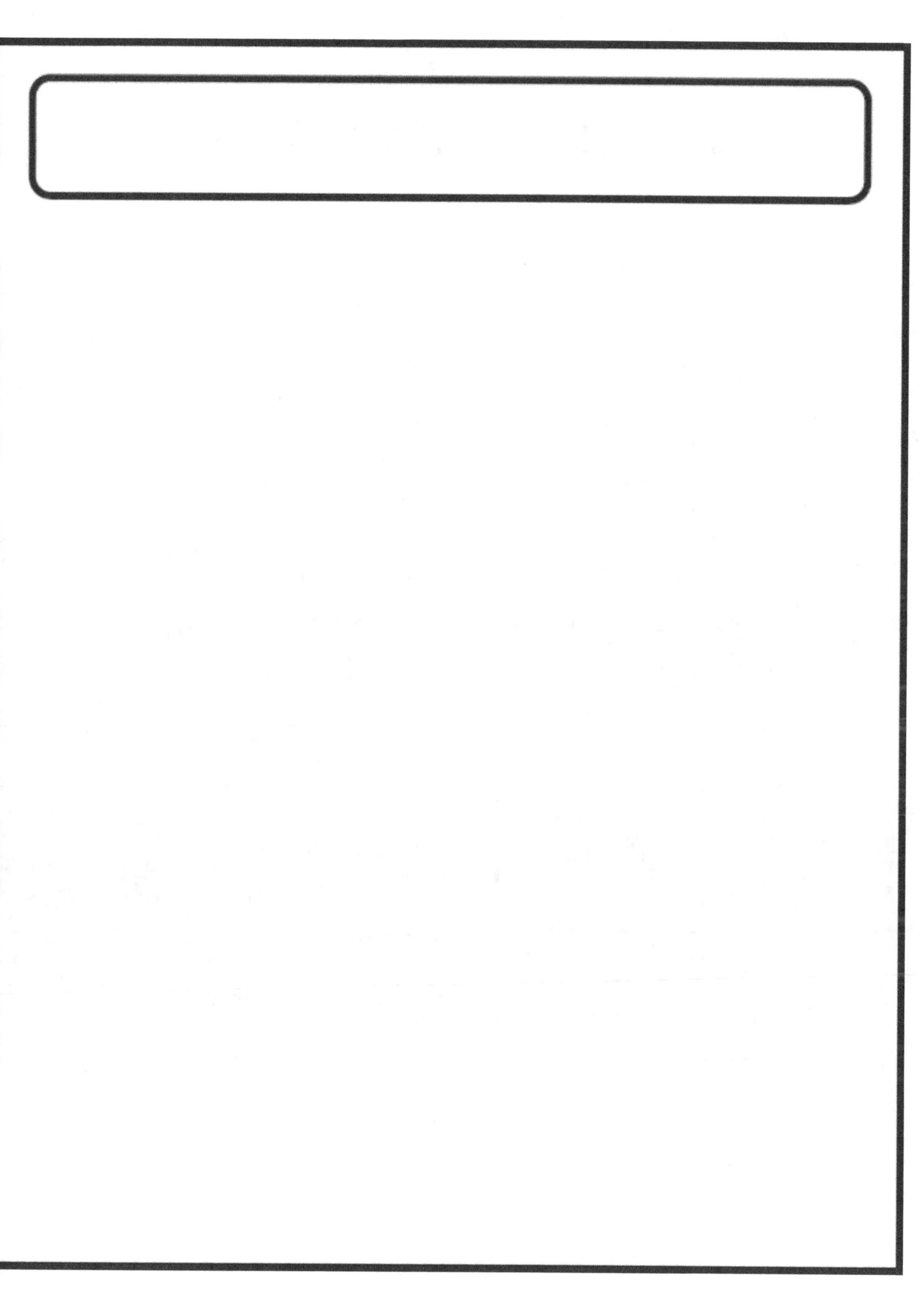

SKYSCRAPERS MALBUCH

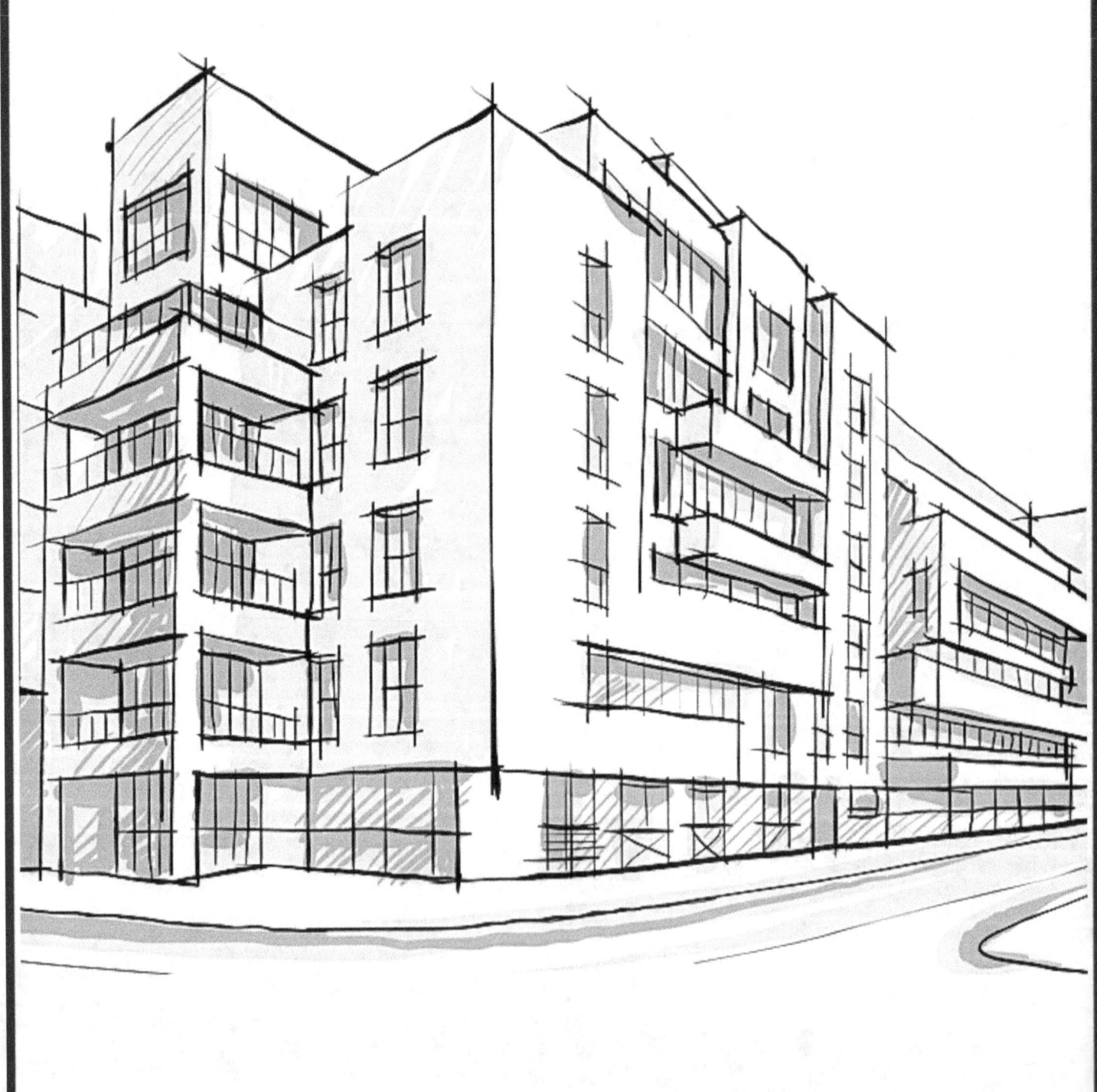

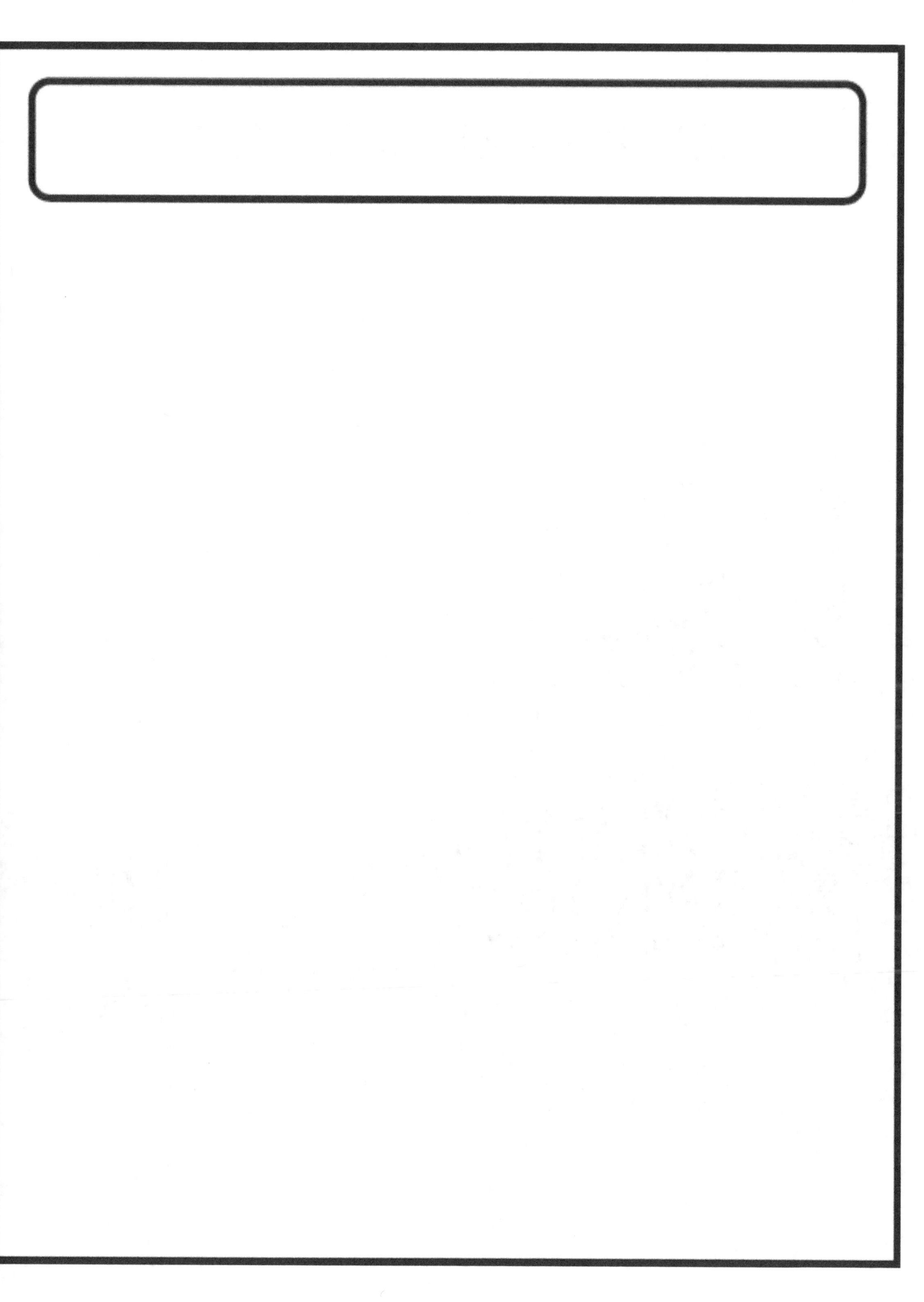

SKYSCRAPERS MALBUCH

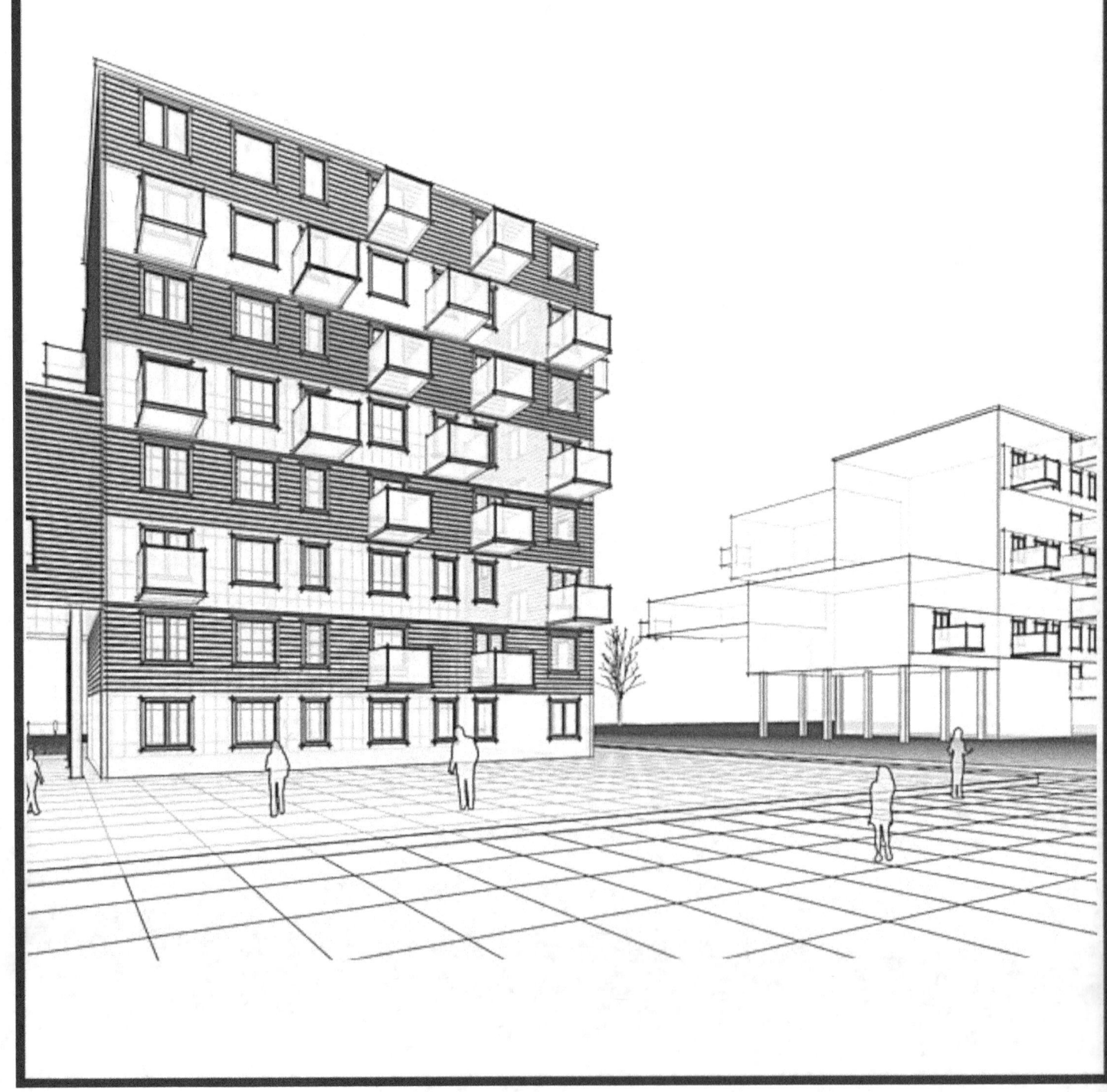

SKYSCRAPERS MALBUCH

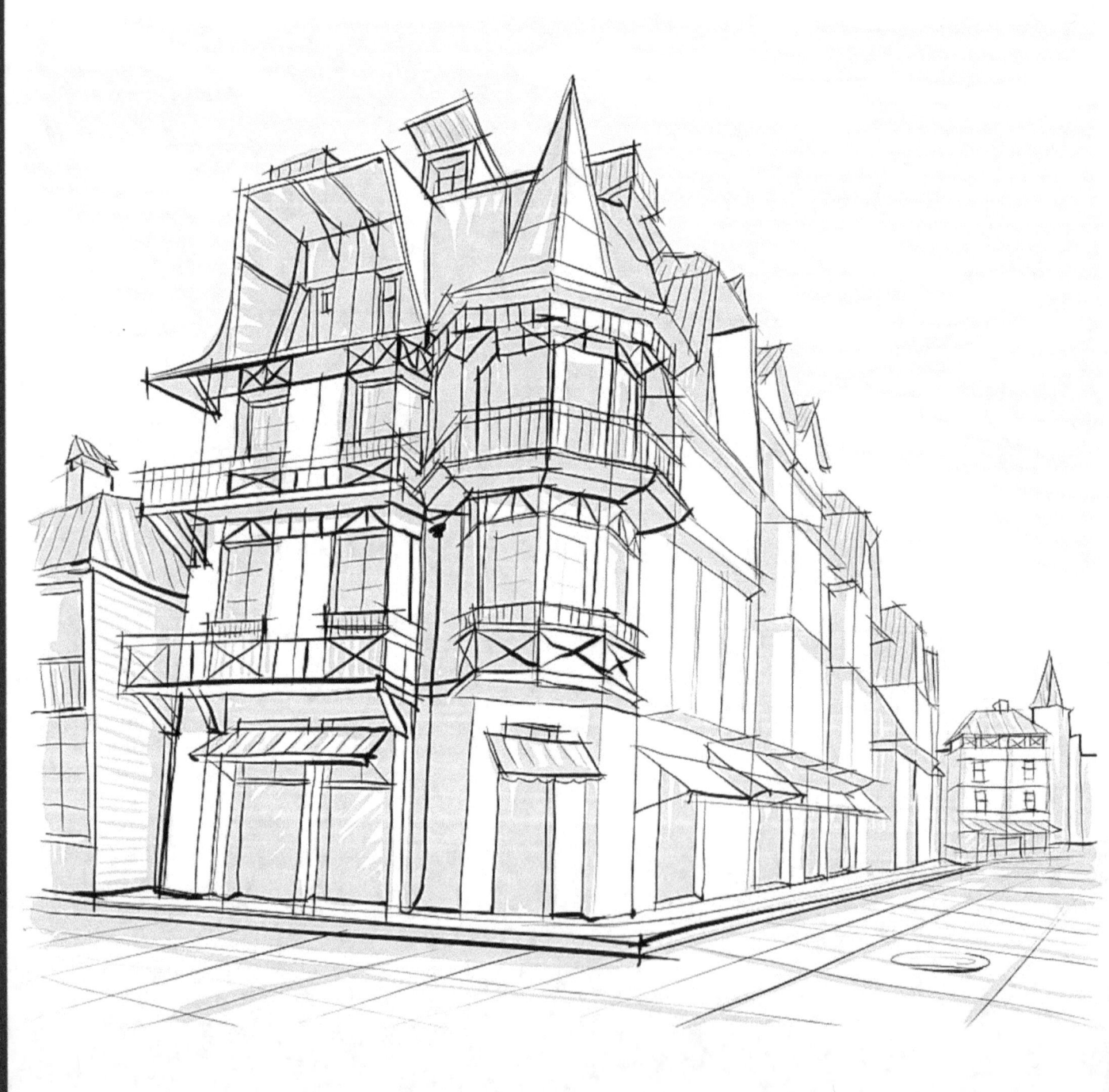

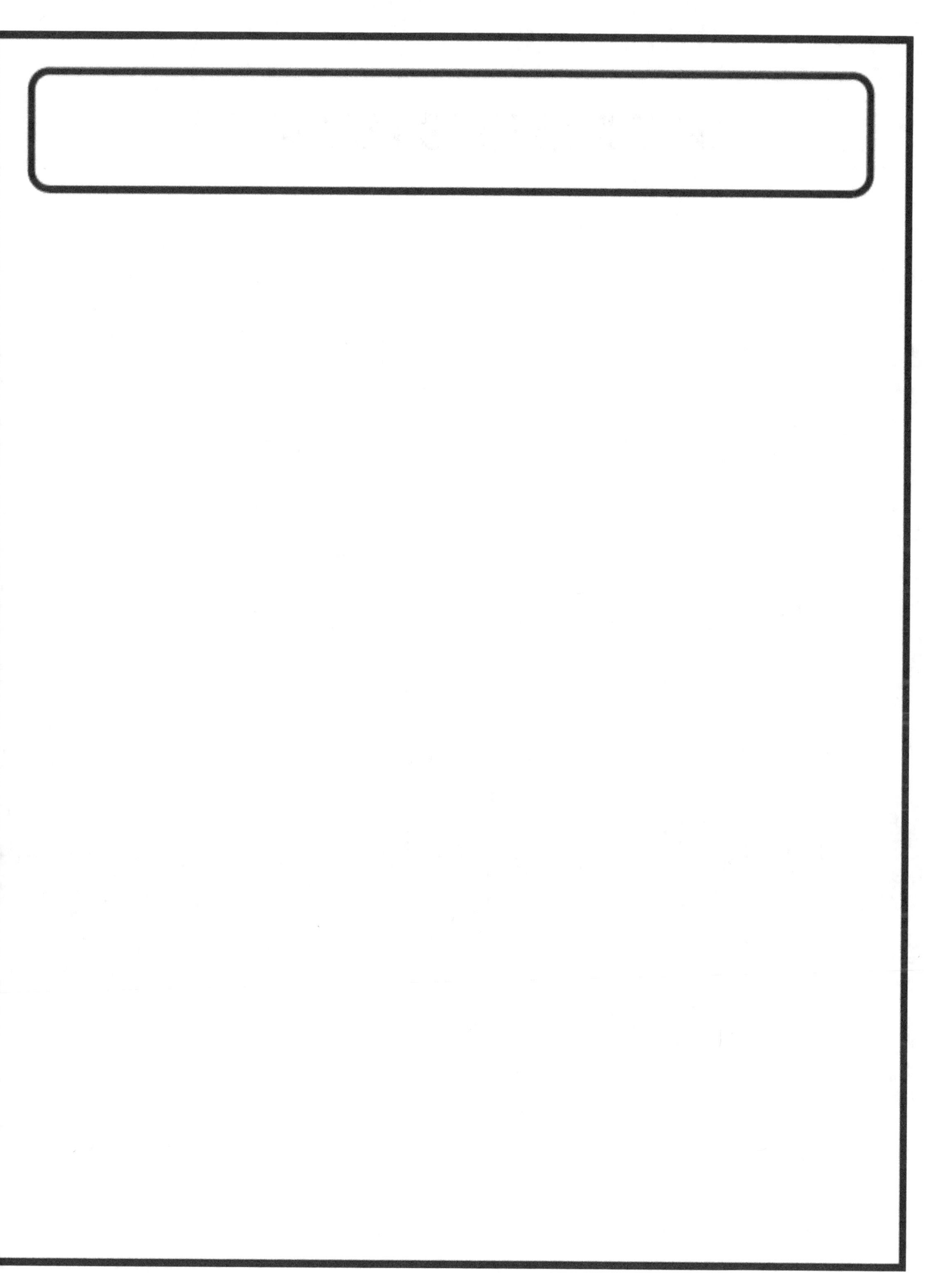

SKYSCRAPERS MALBUCH

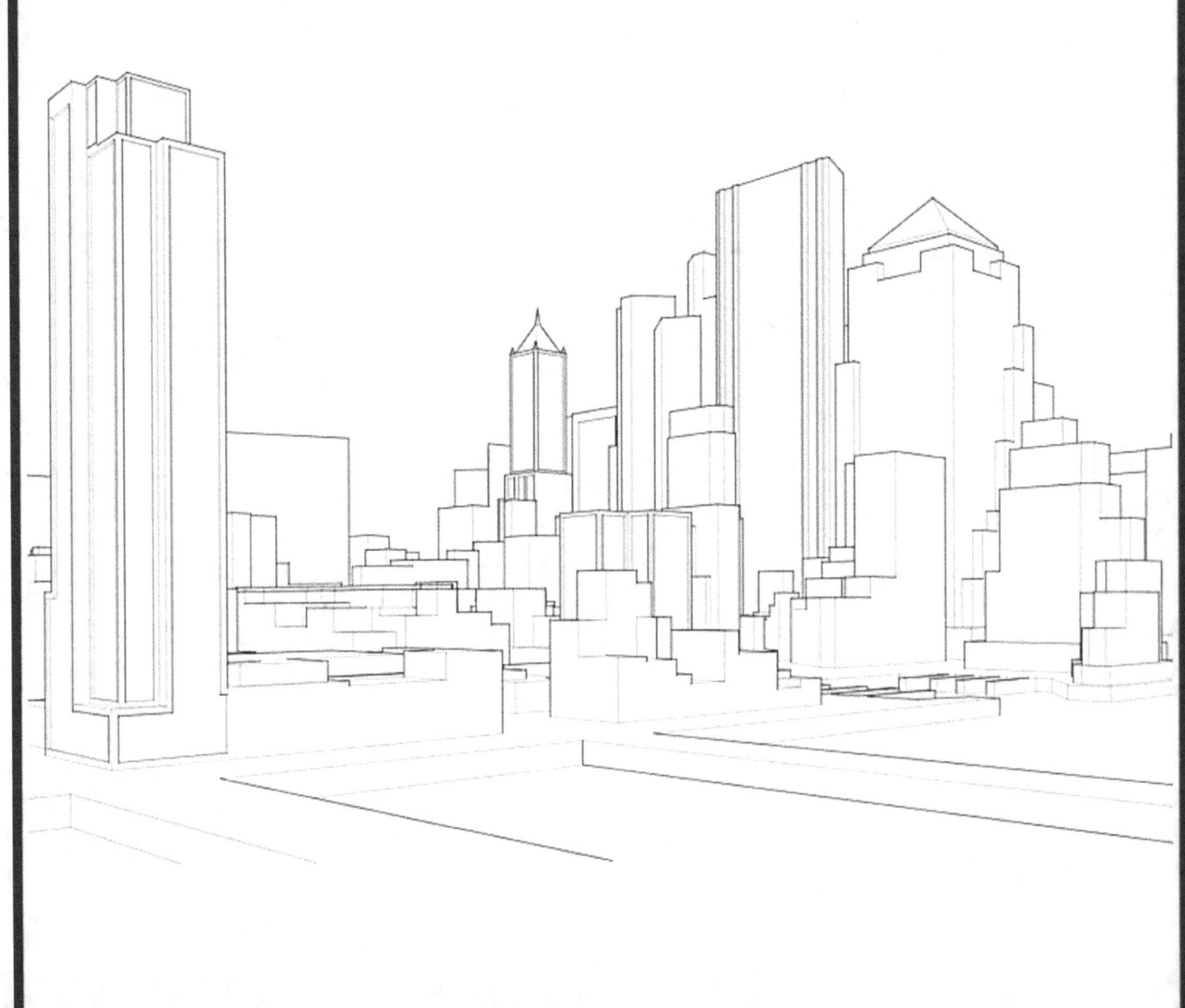

SKYSCRAPERS MALBUCH

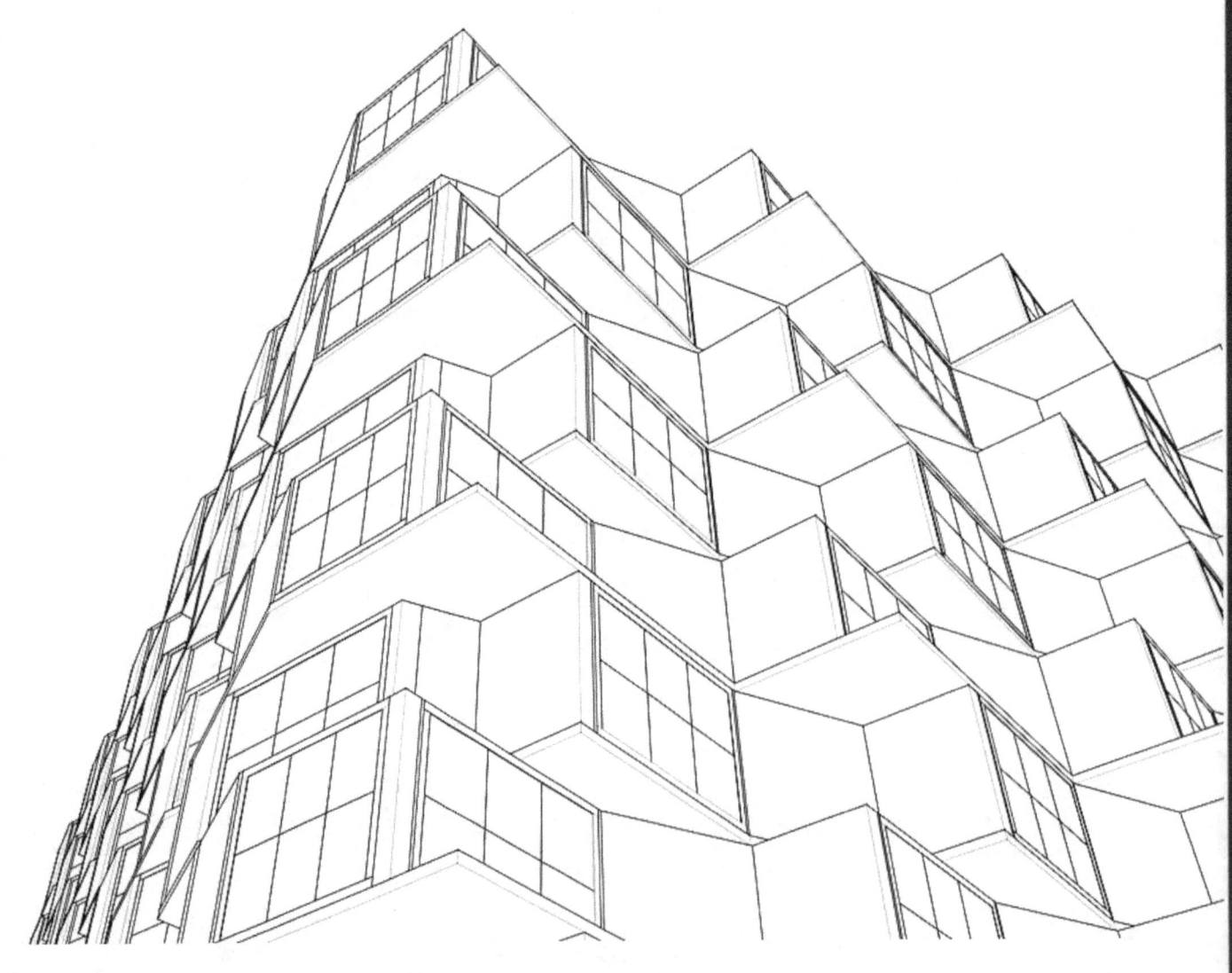

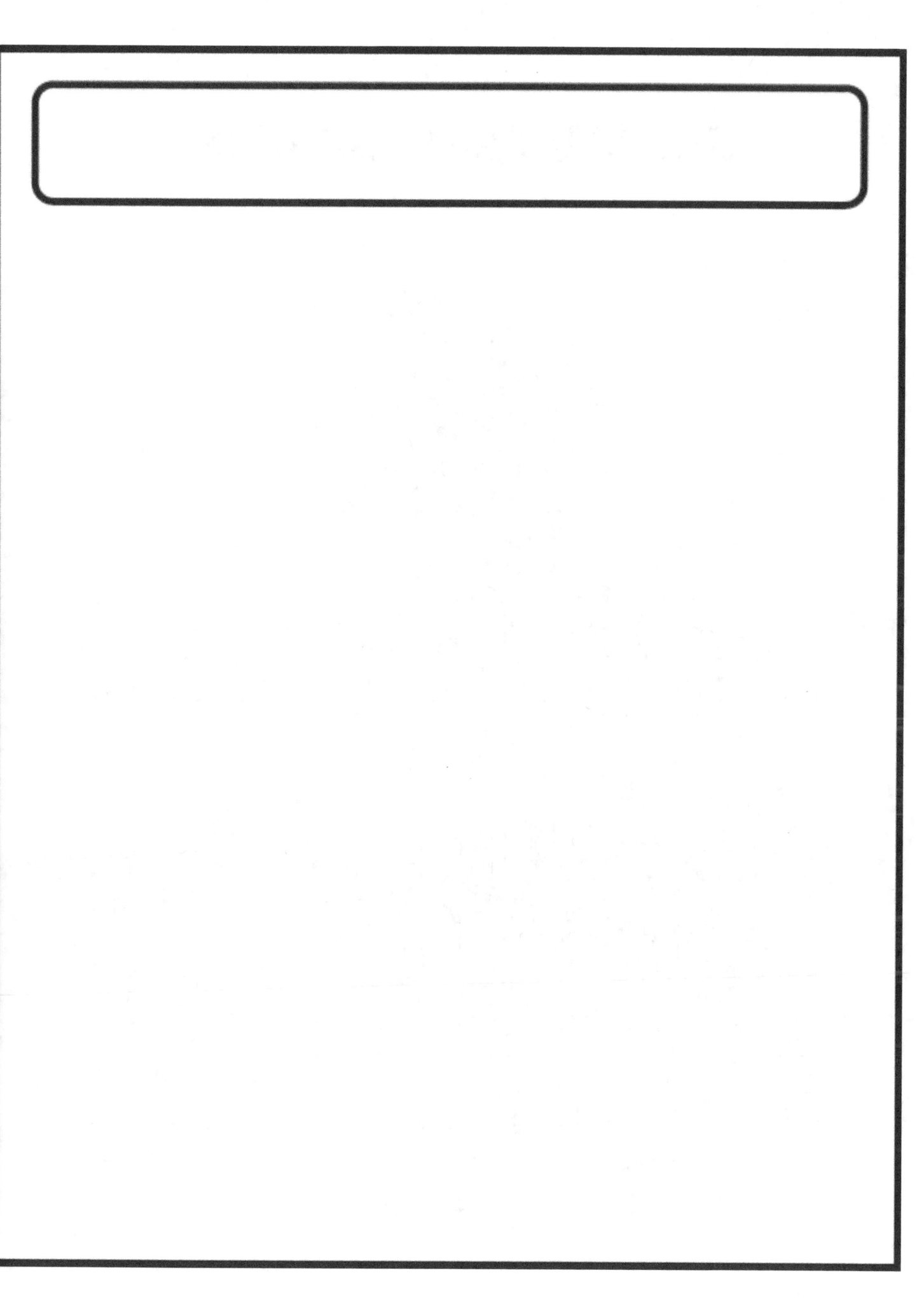

SKYSCRAPERS MALBUCH

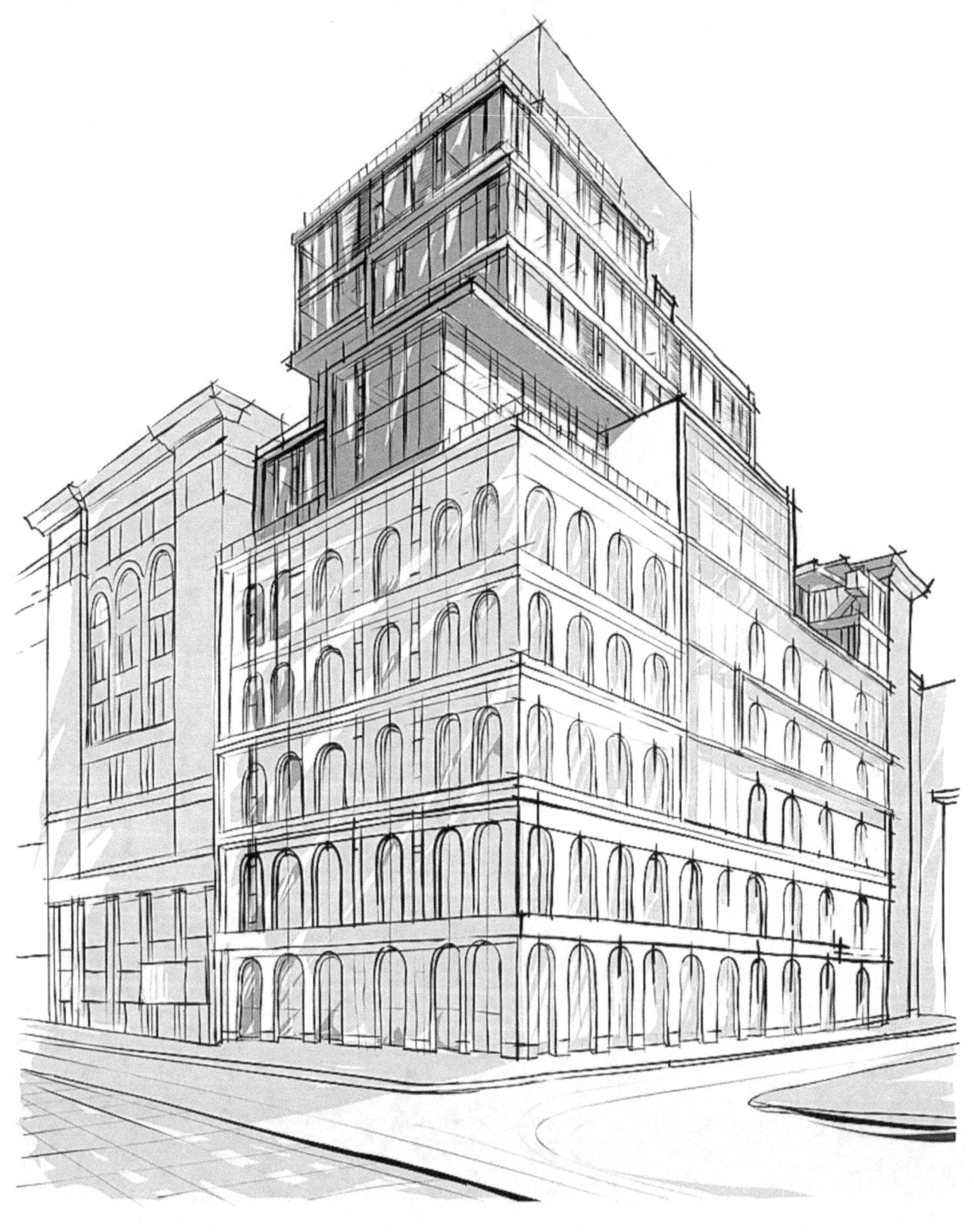

SKYSCRAPERS MALBUCH

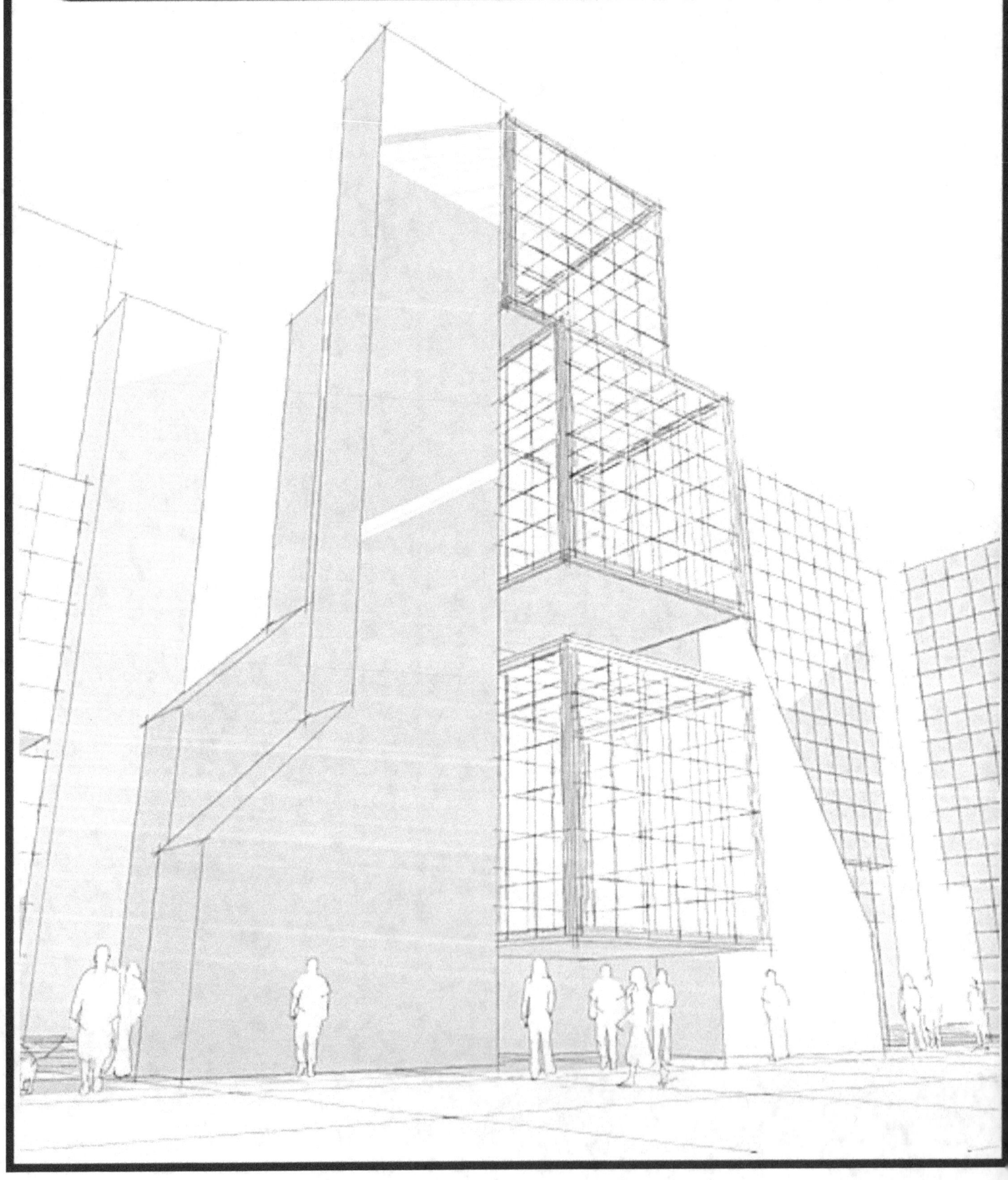

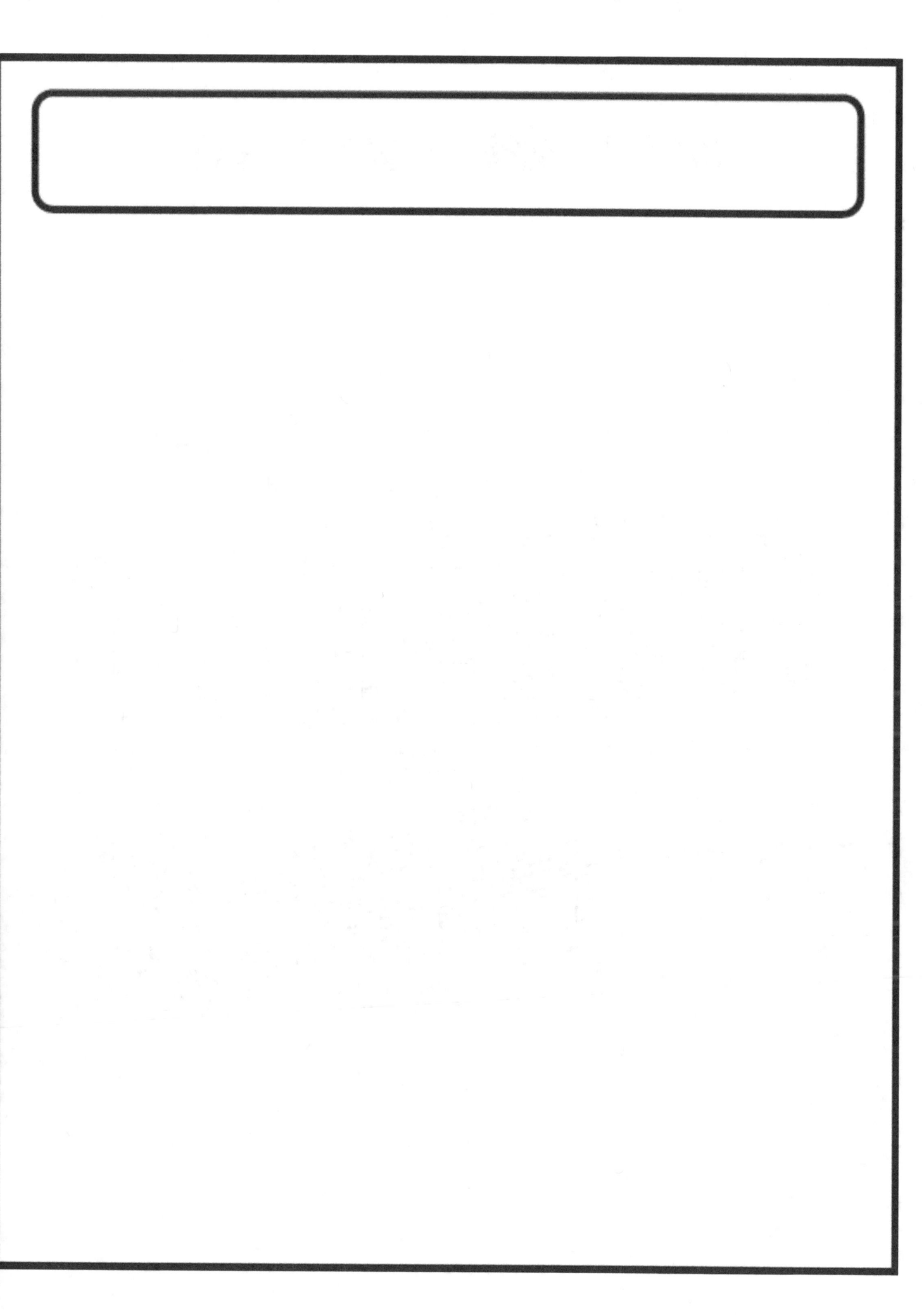

SKYSCRAPERS MALBUCH

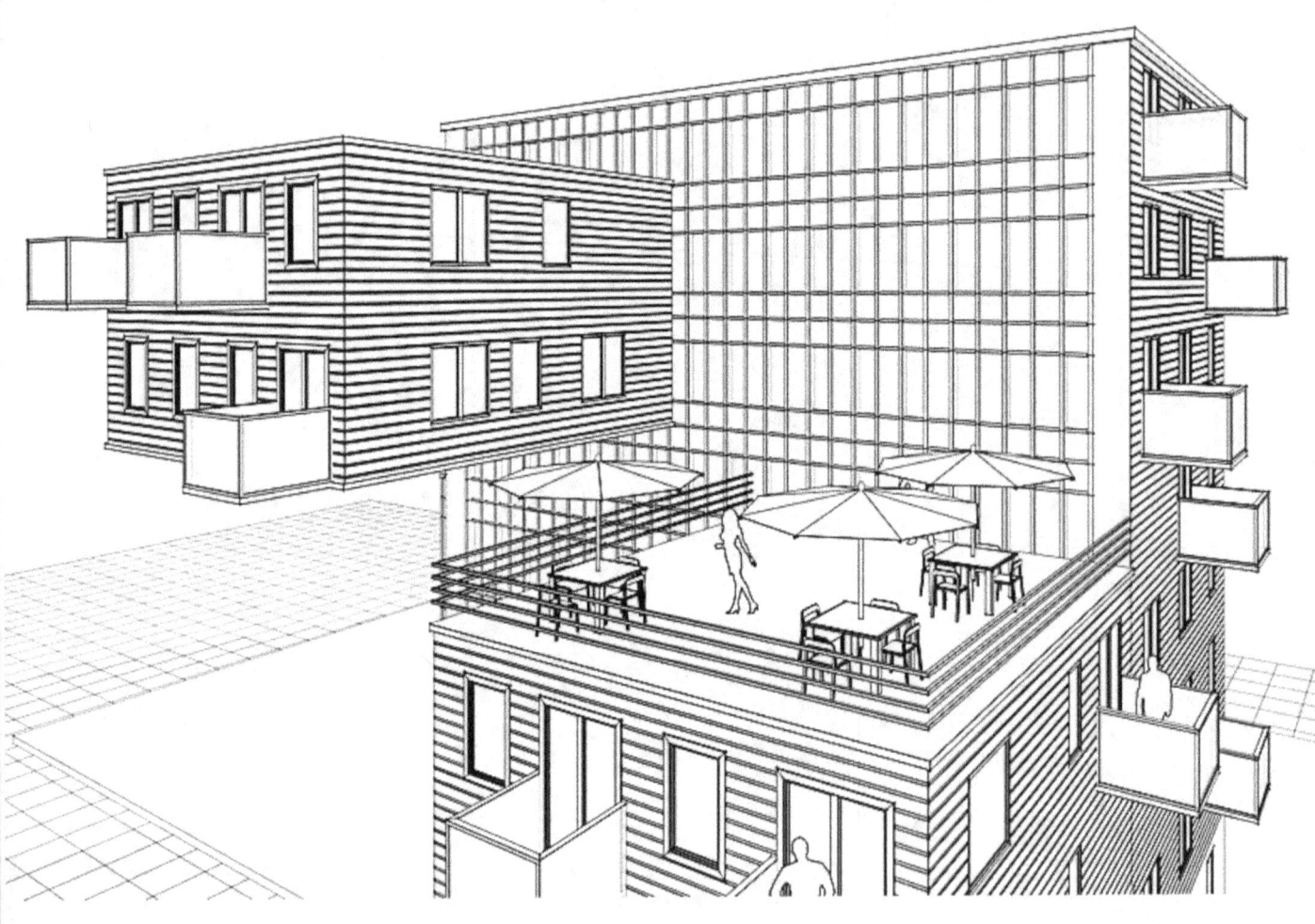

SKYSCRAPERS MALBUCH

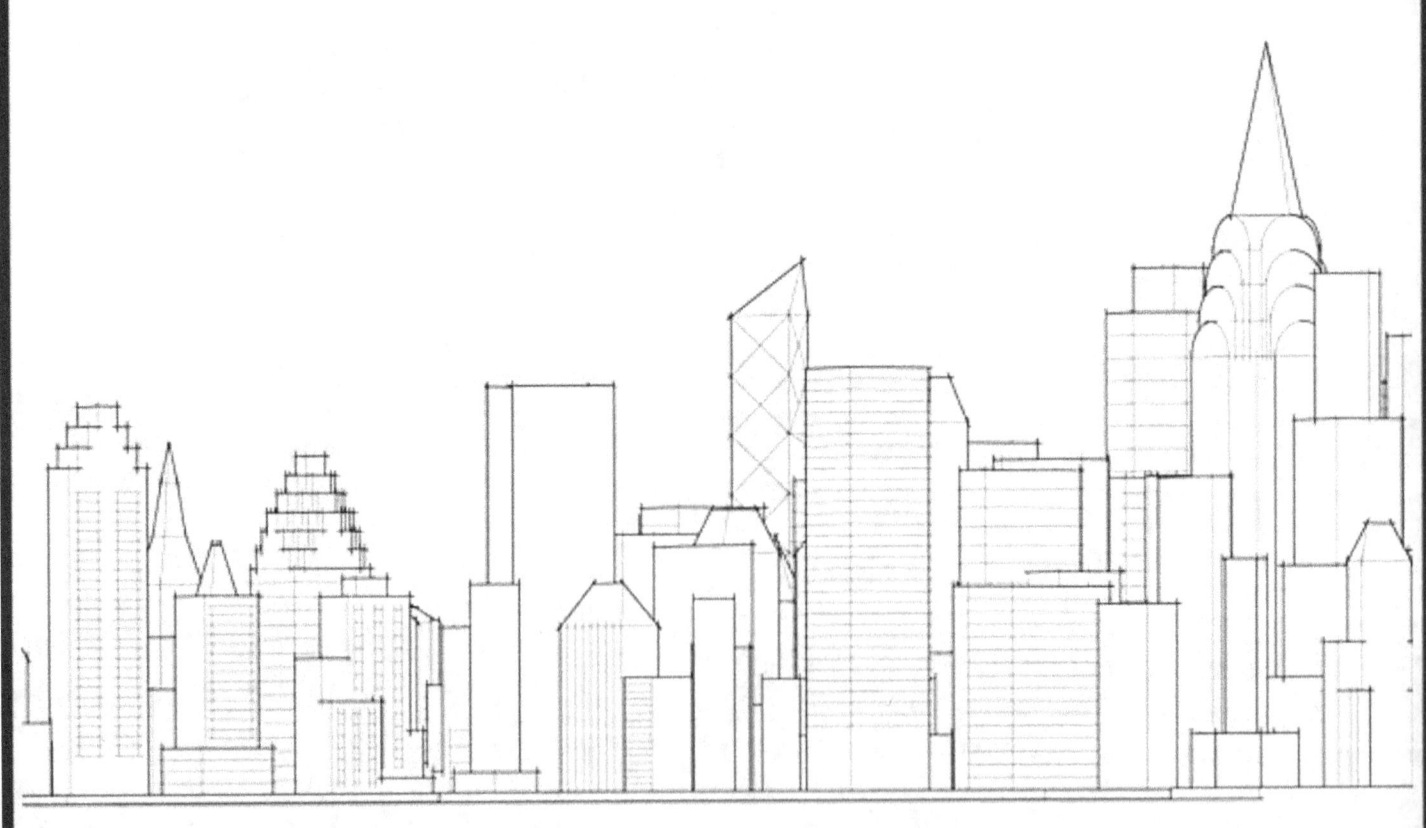

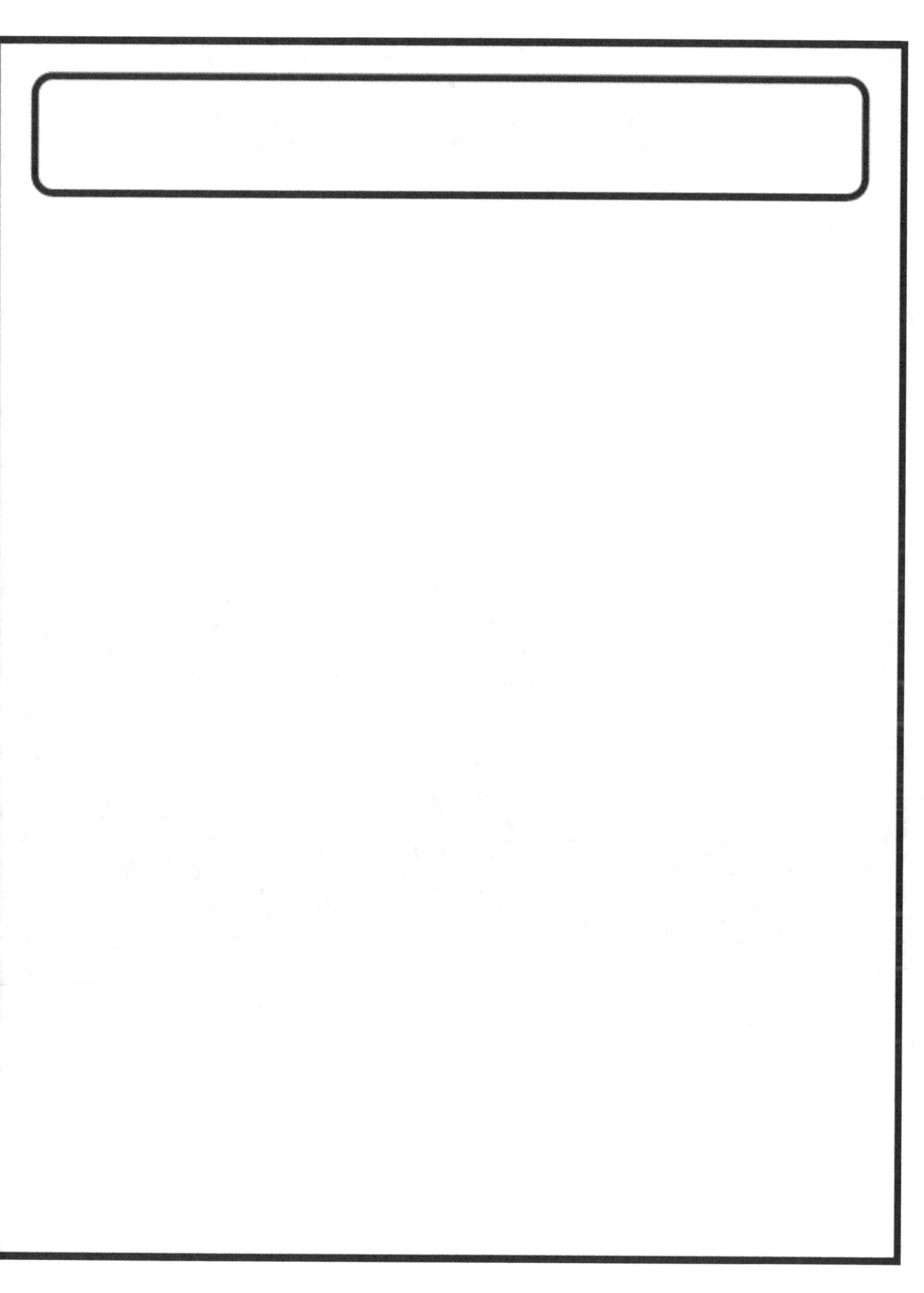

SKYSCRAPERS MALBUCH

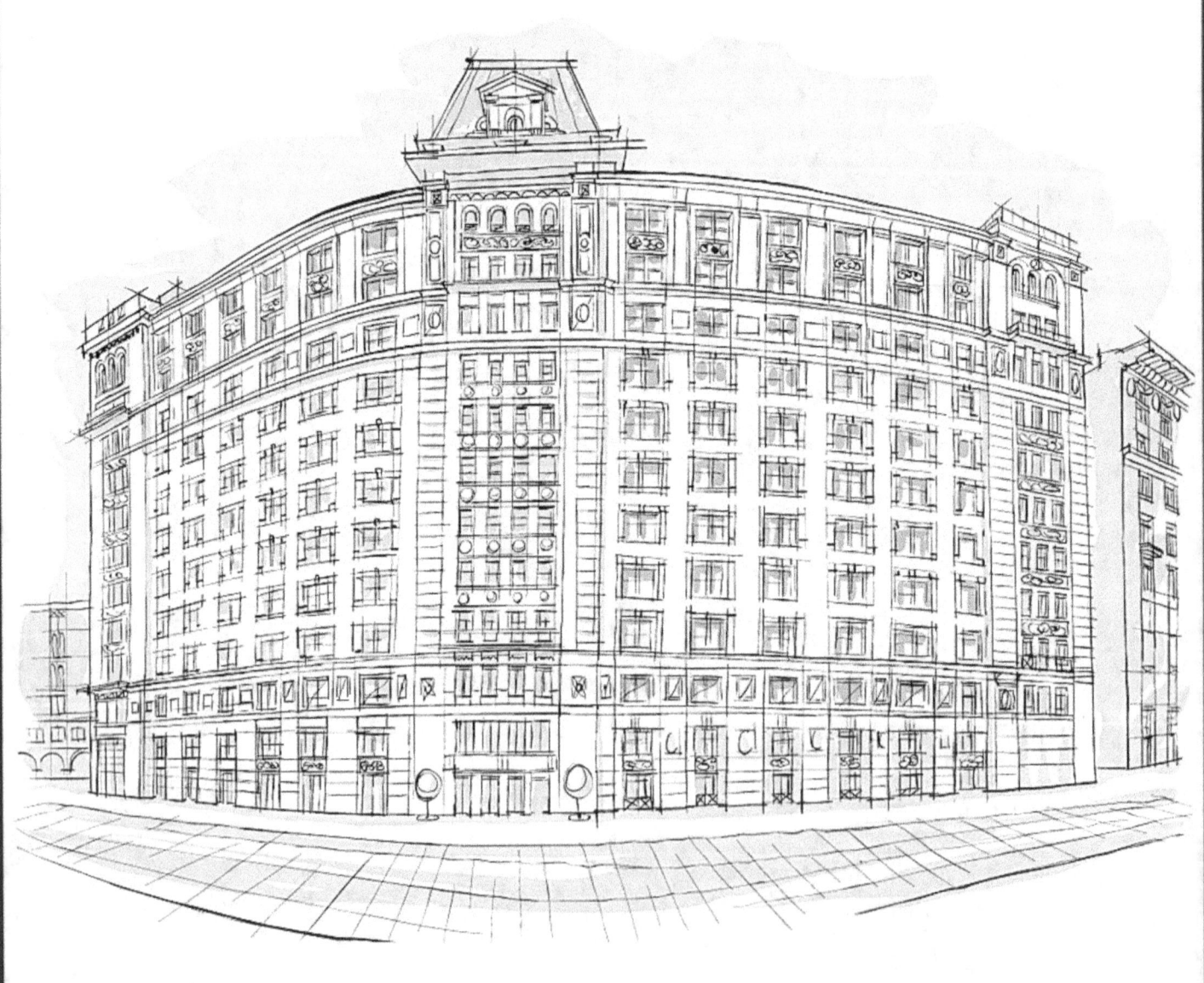

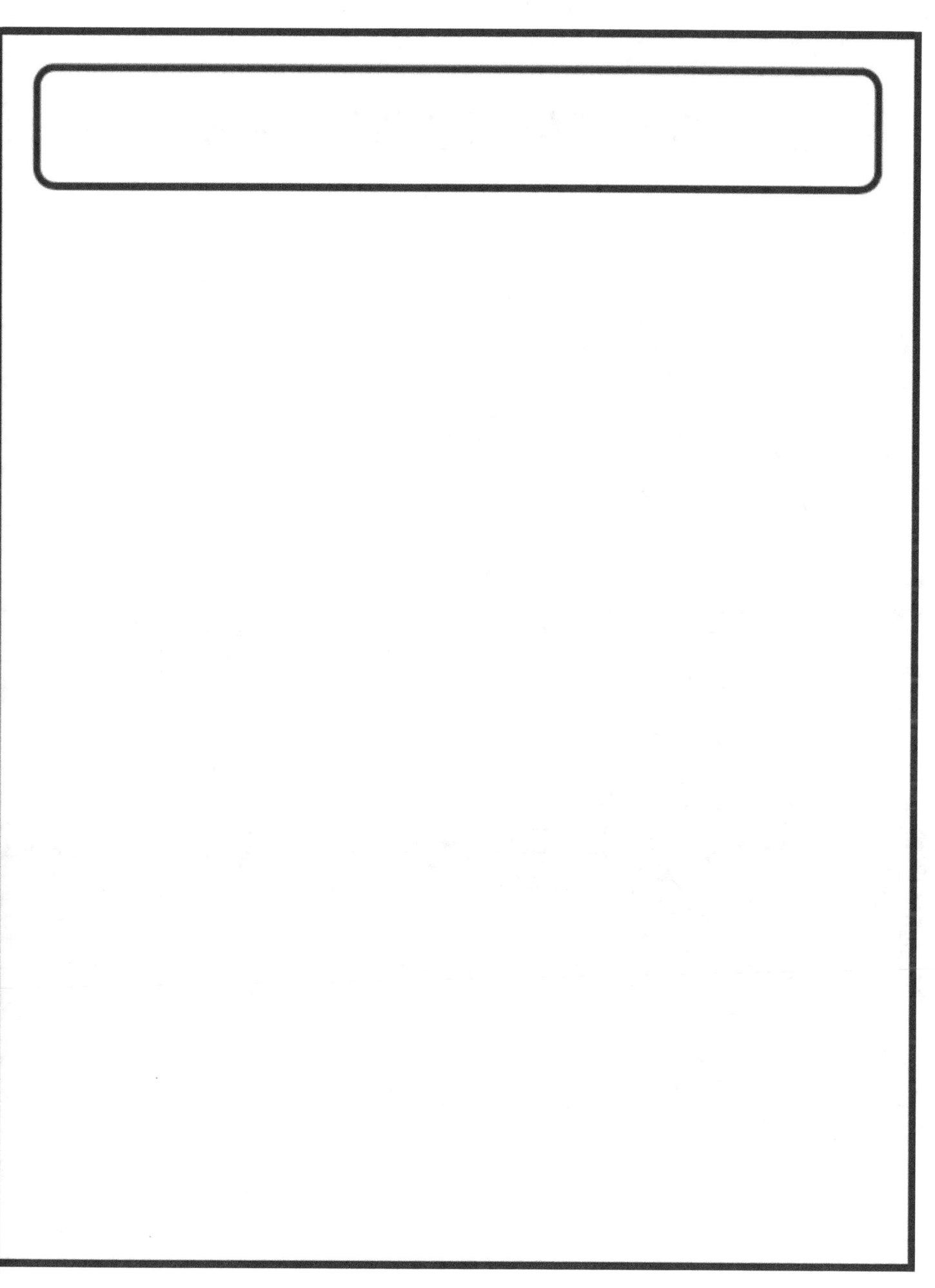

SKYSCRAPERS MALBUCH

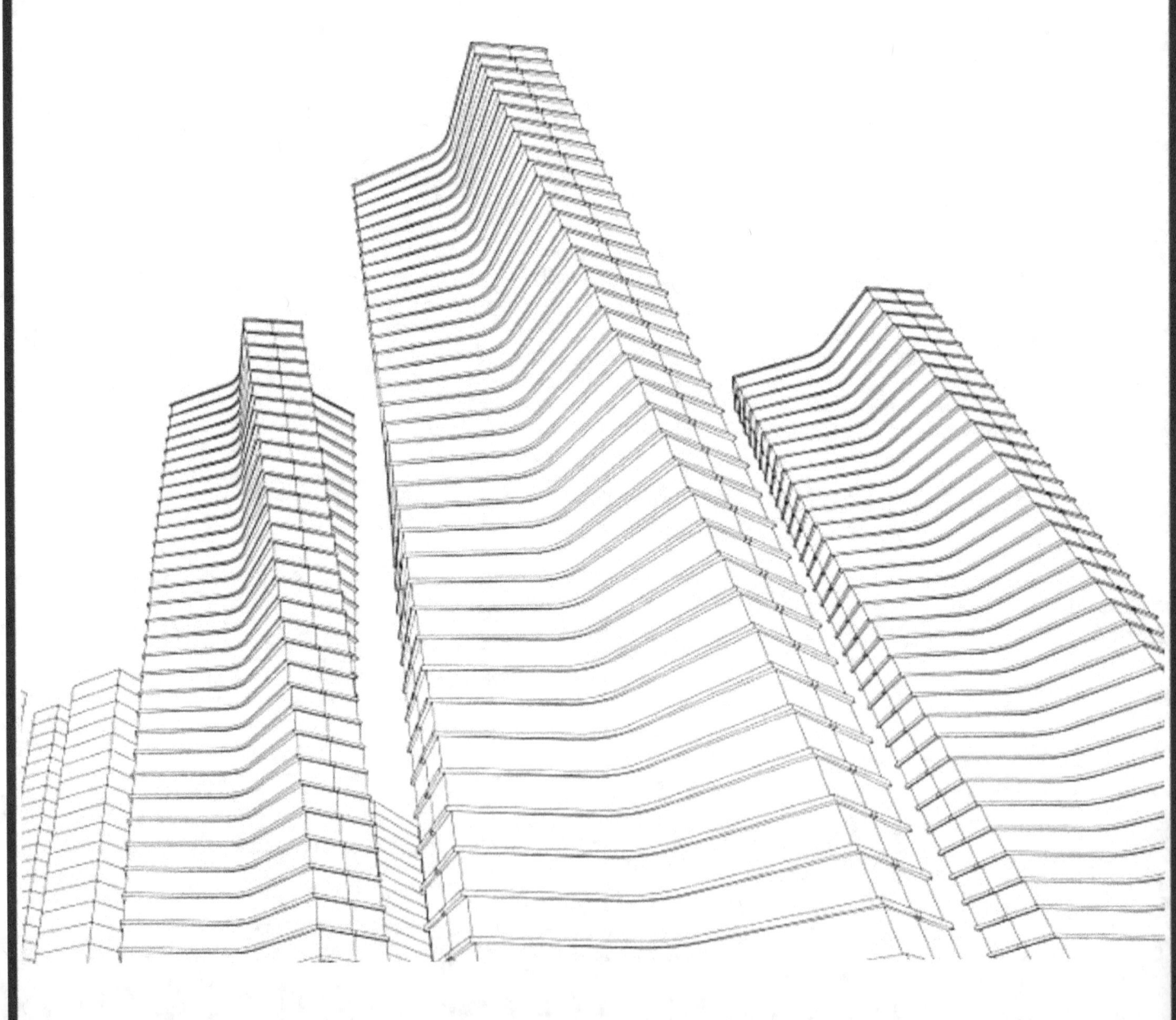

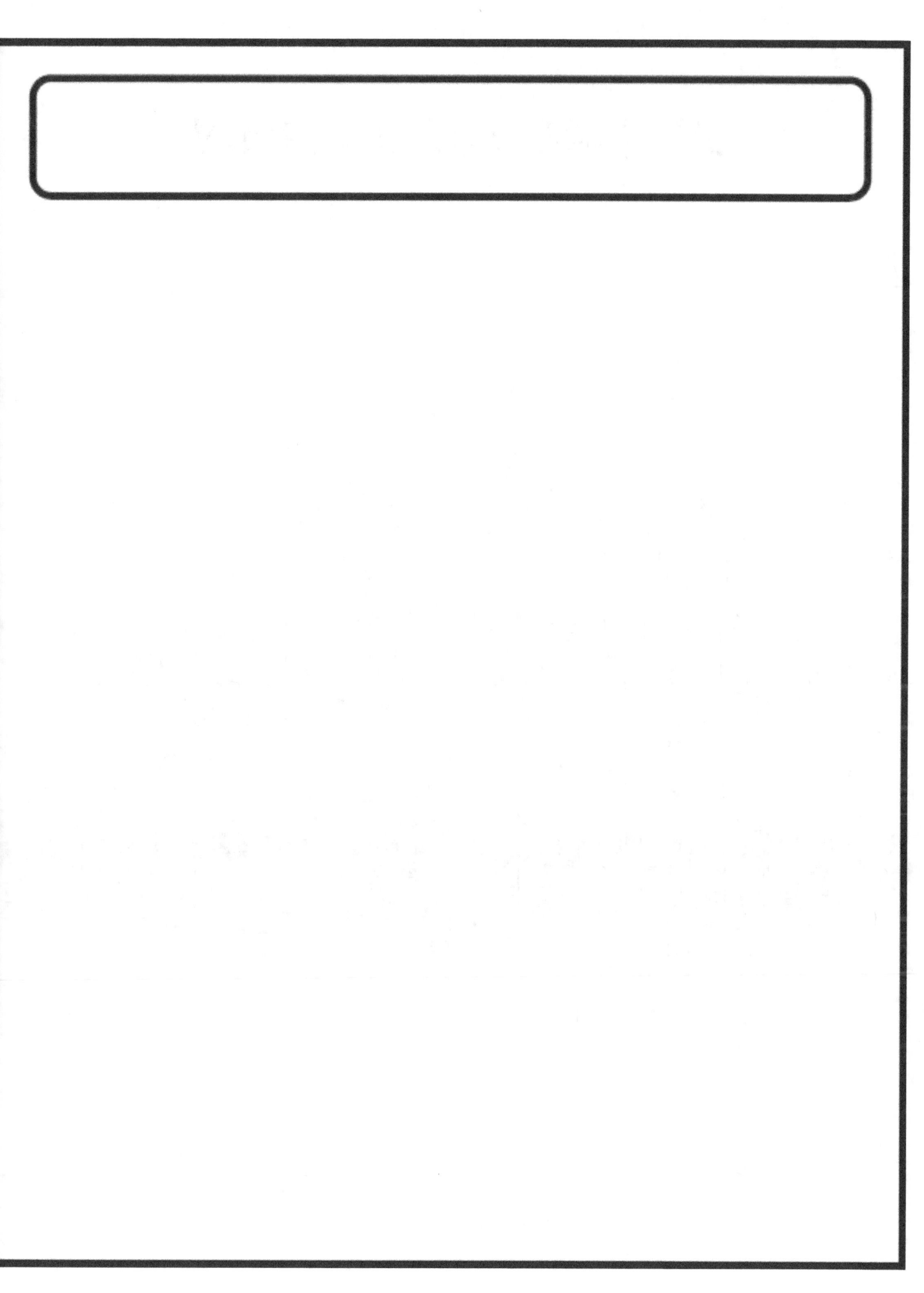

SKYSCRAPERS MALBUCH

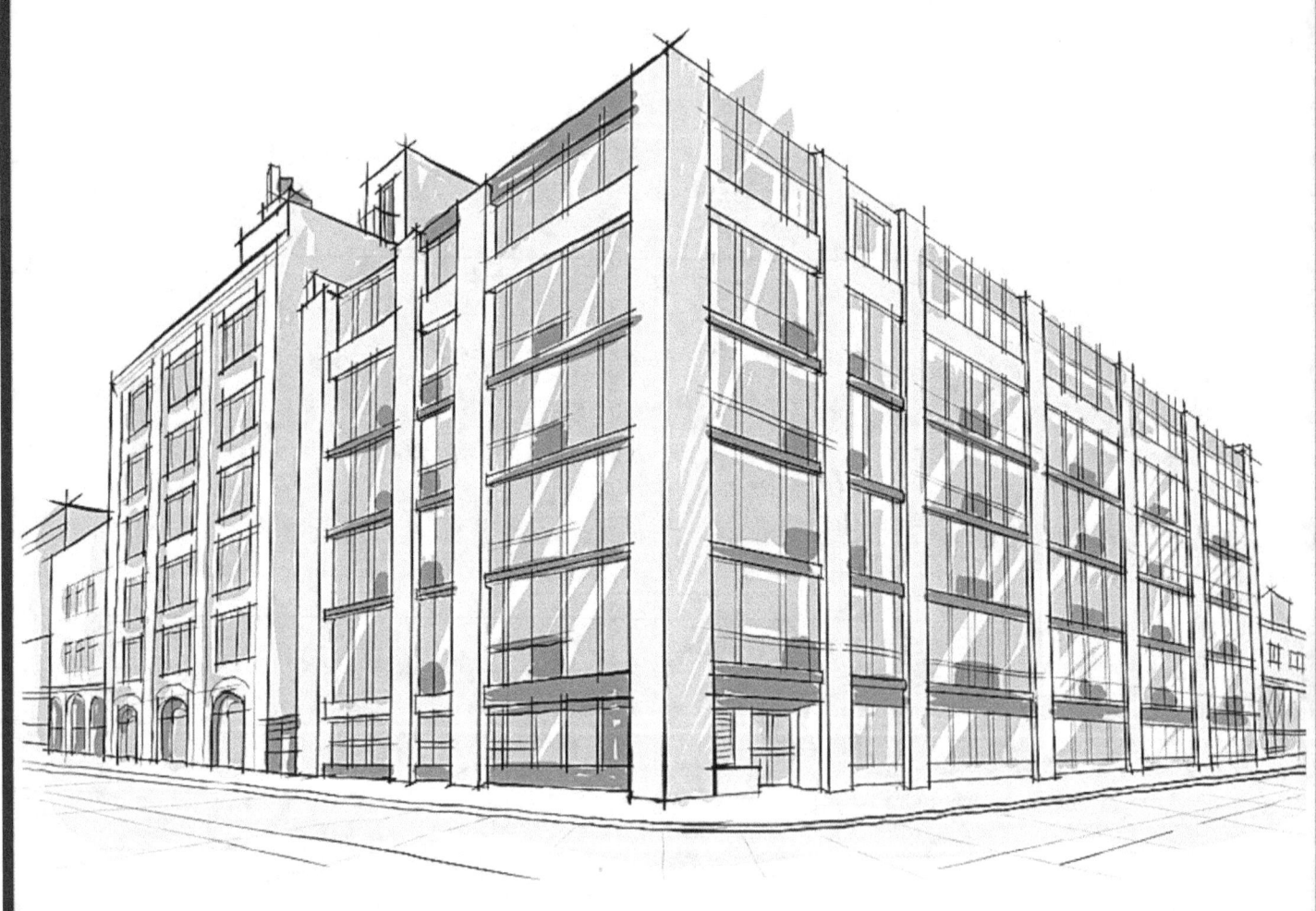

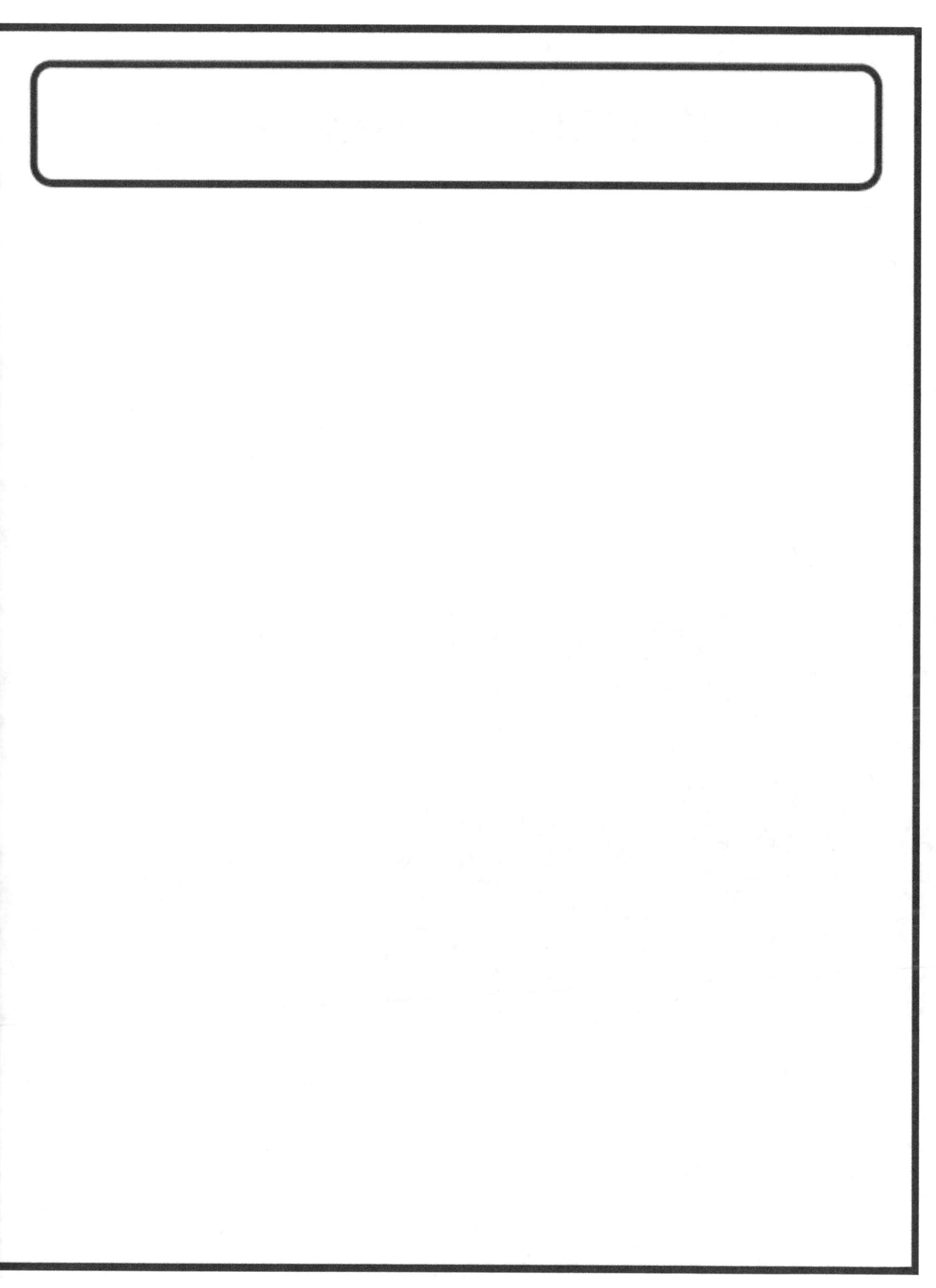

SKYSCRAPERS MALBUCH

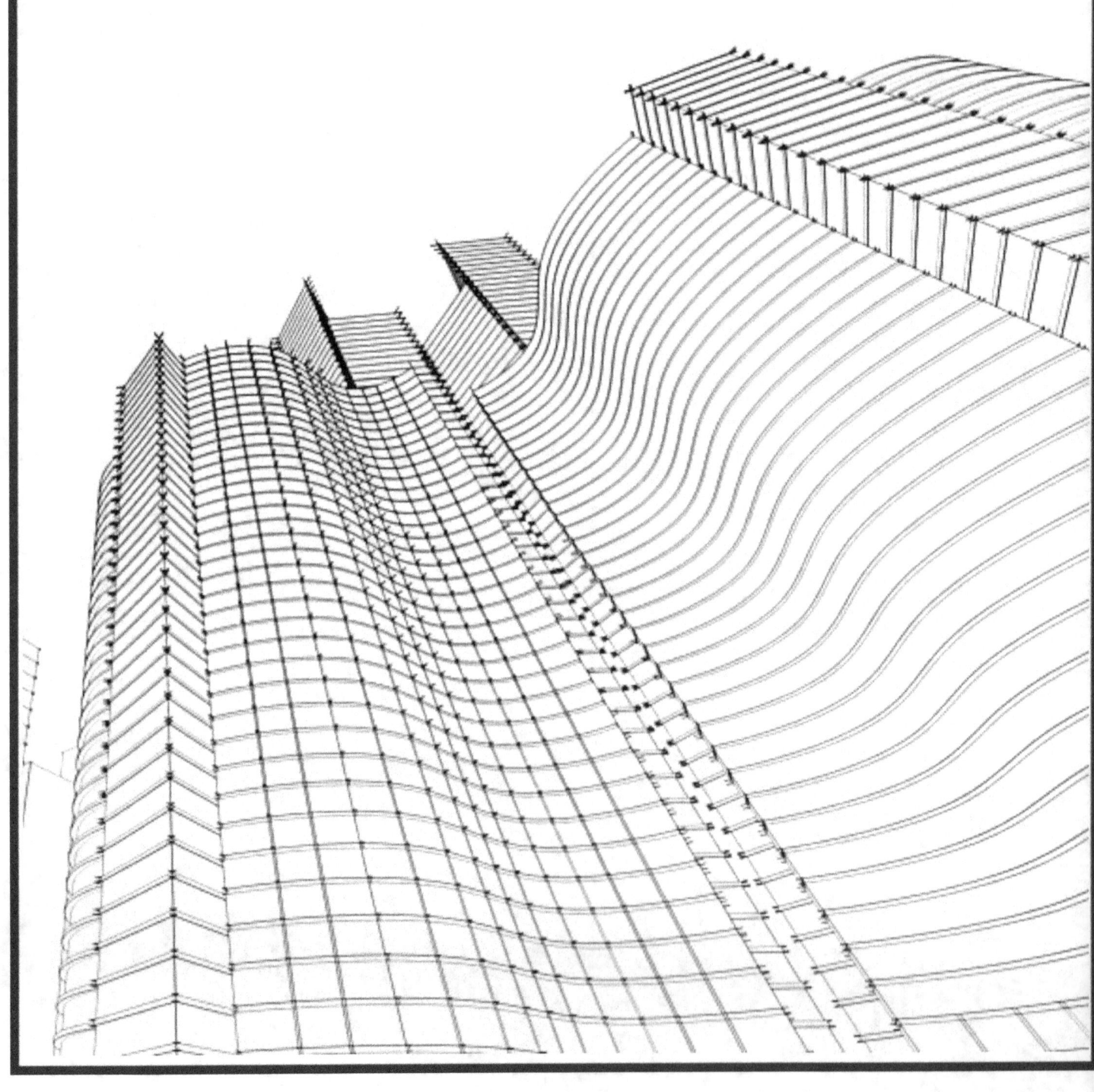

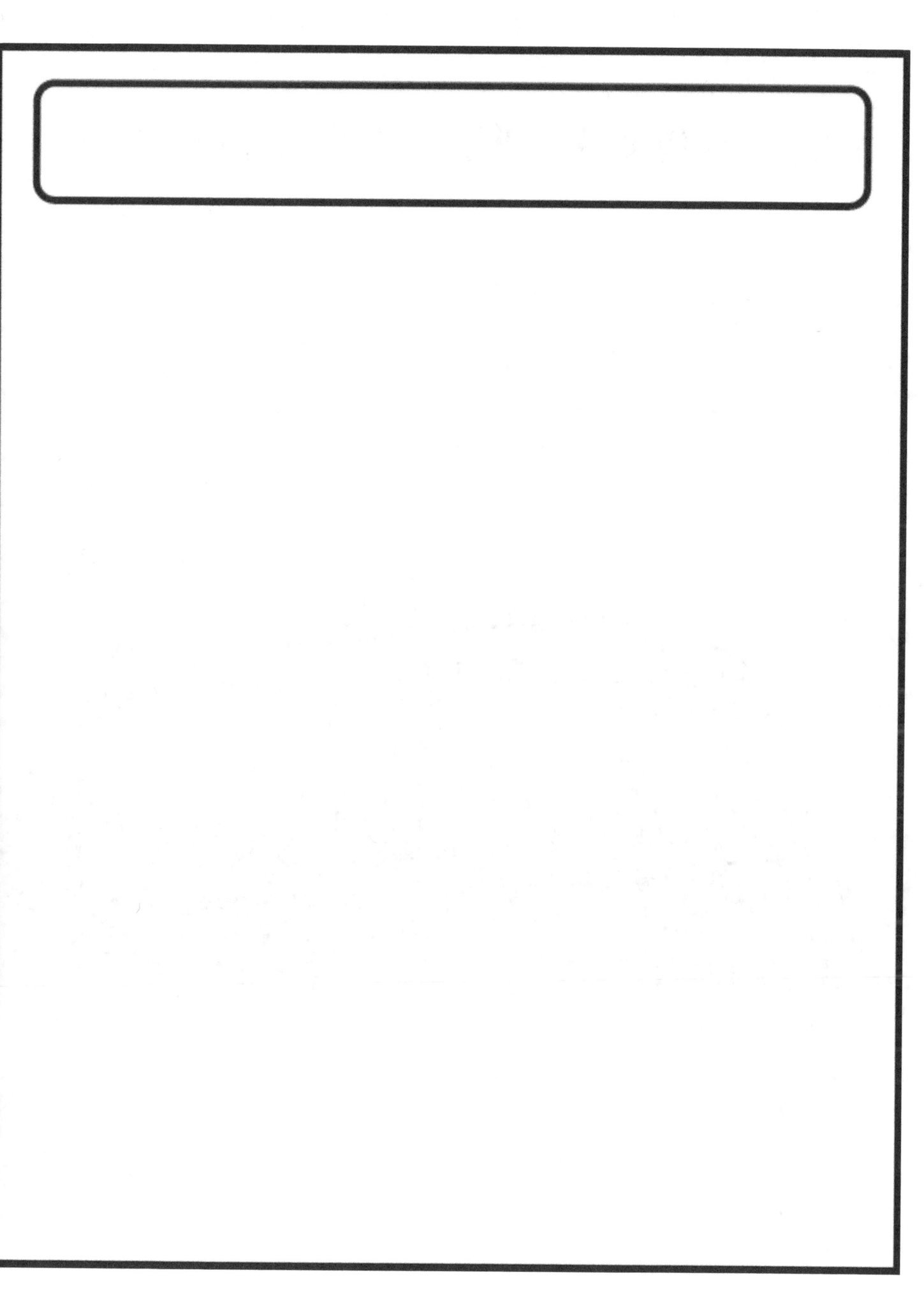

SKYSCRAPERS MALBUCH

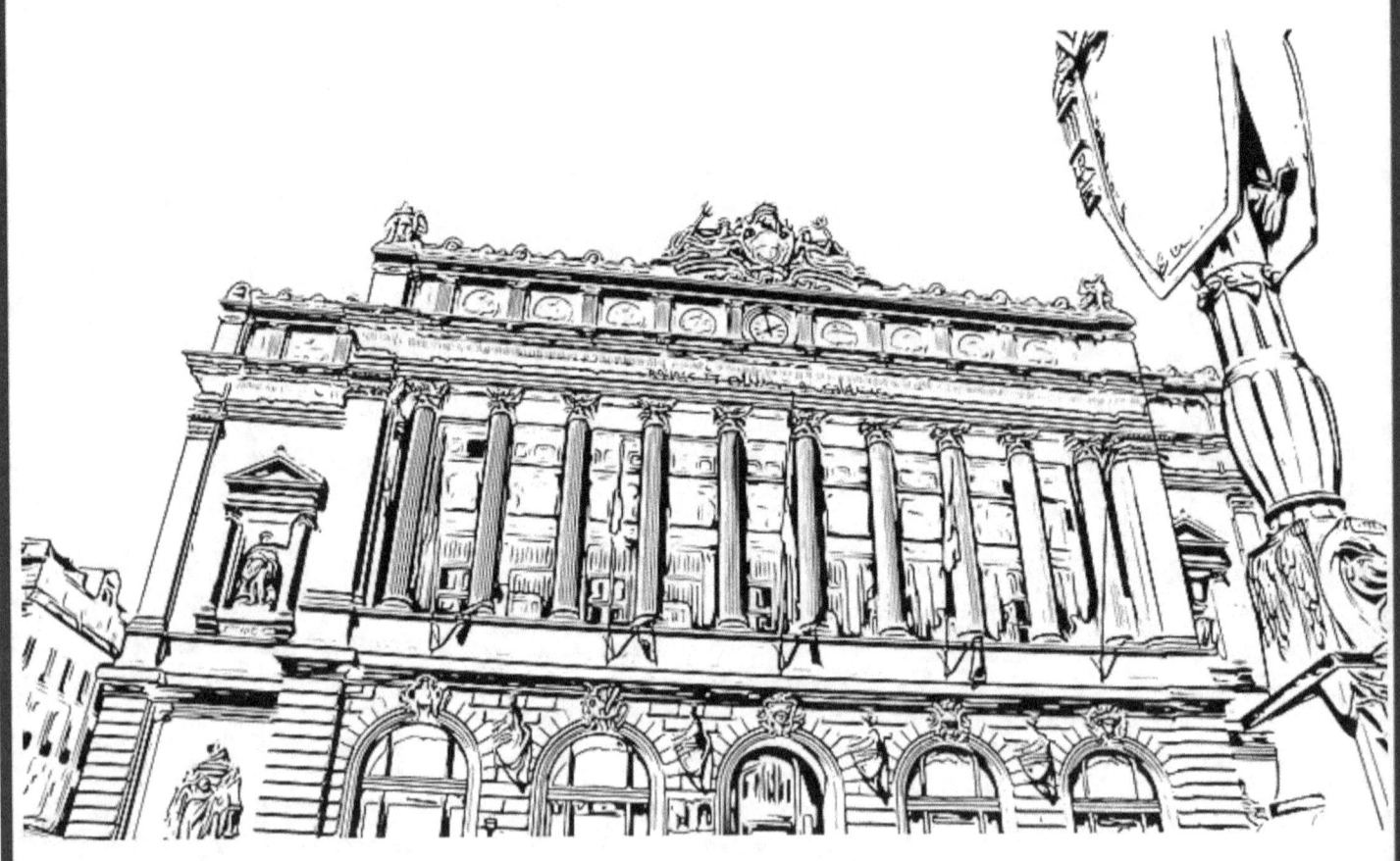

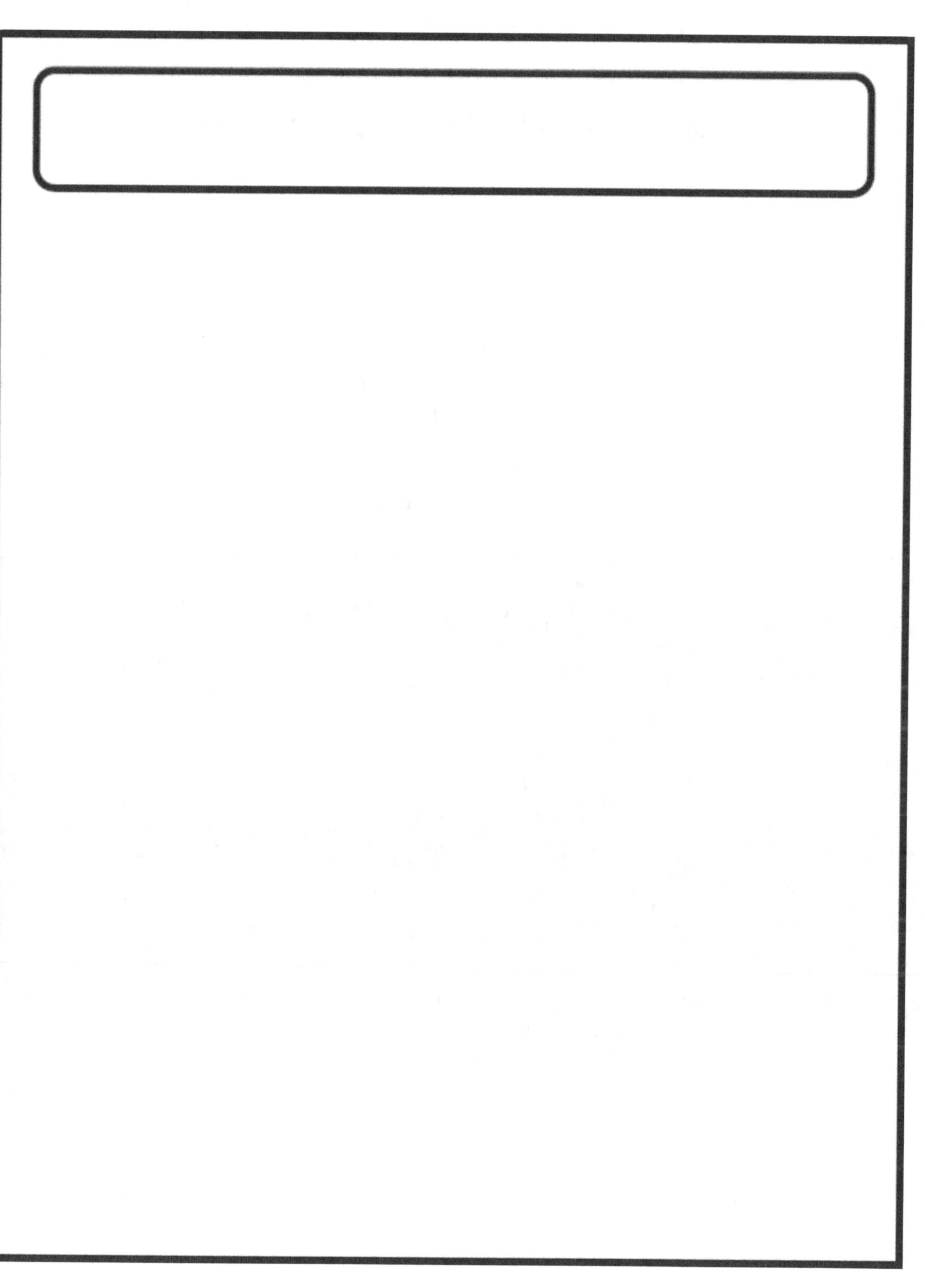

SKYSCRAPERS MALBUCH

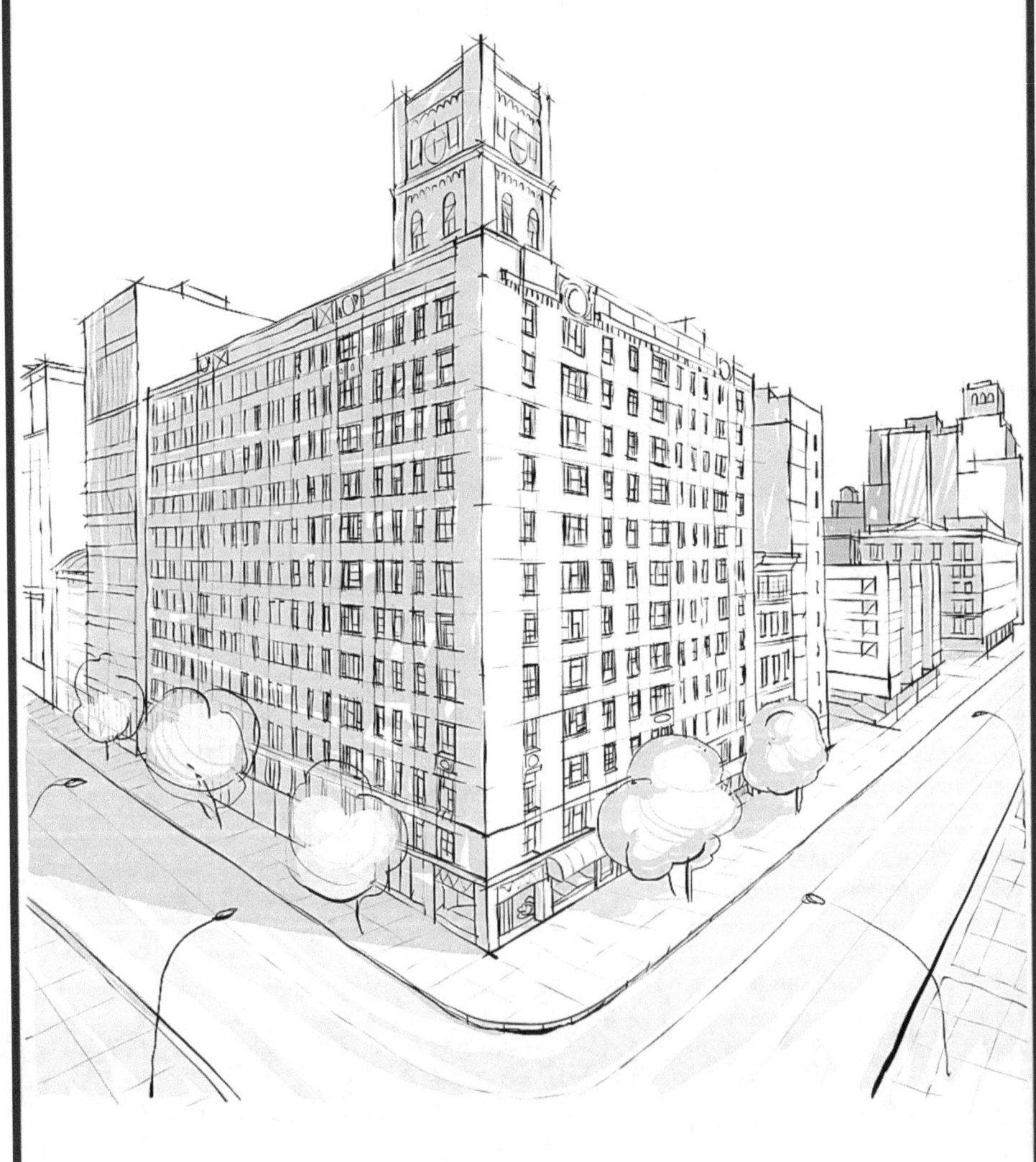

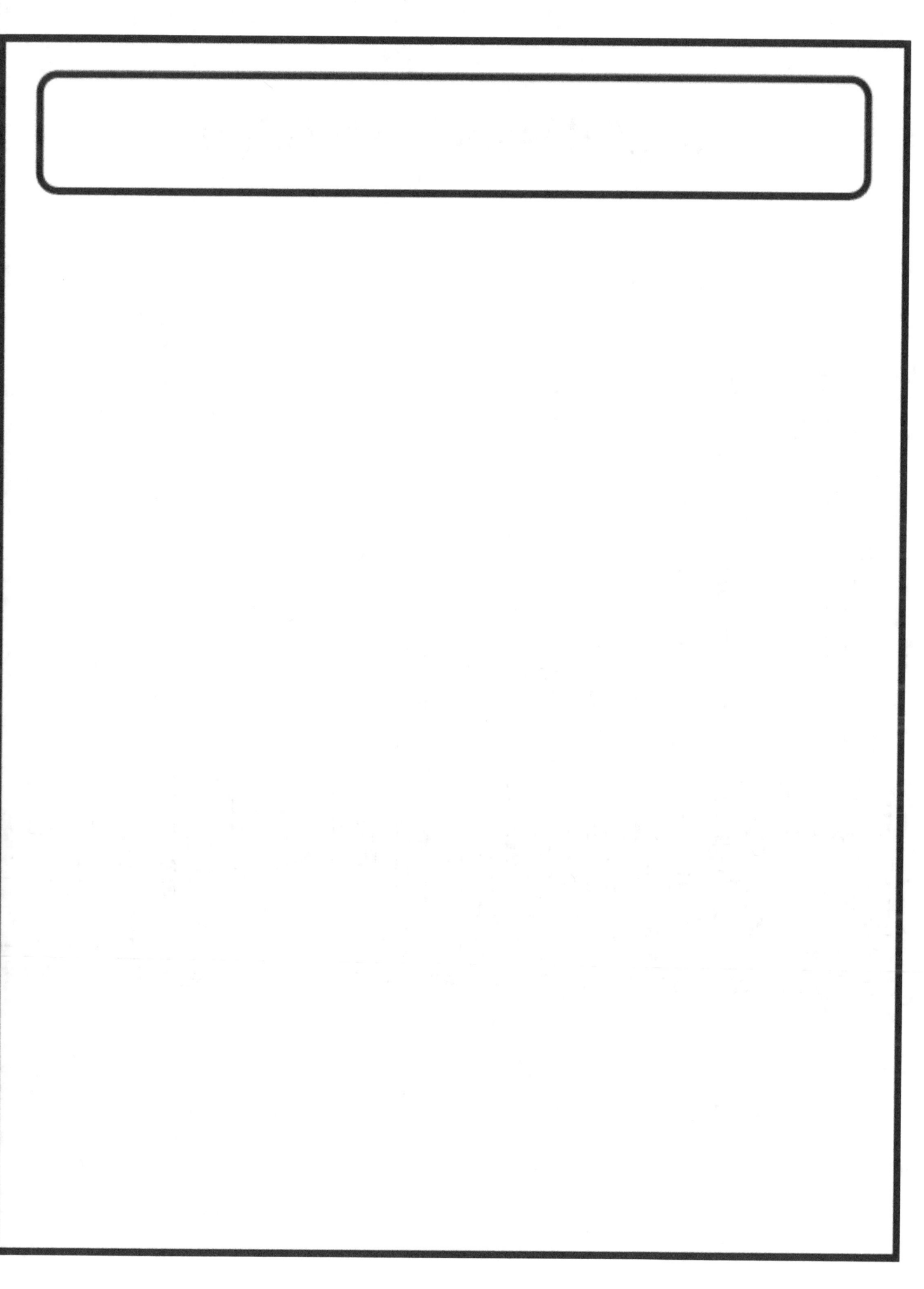

SKYSCRAPERS MALBUCH

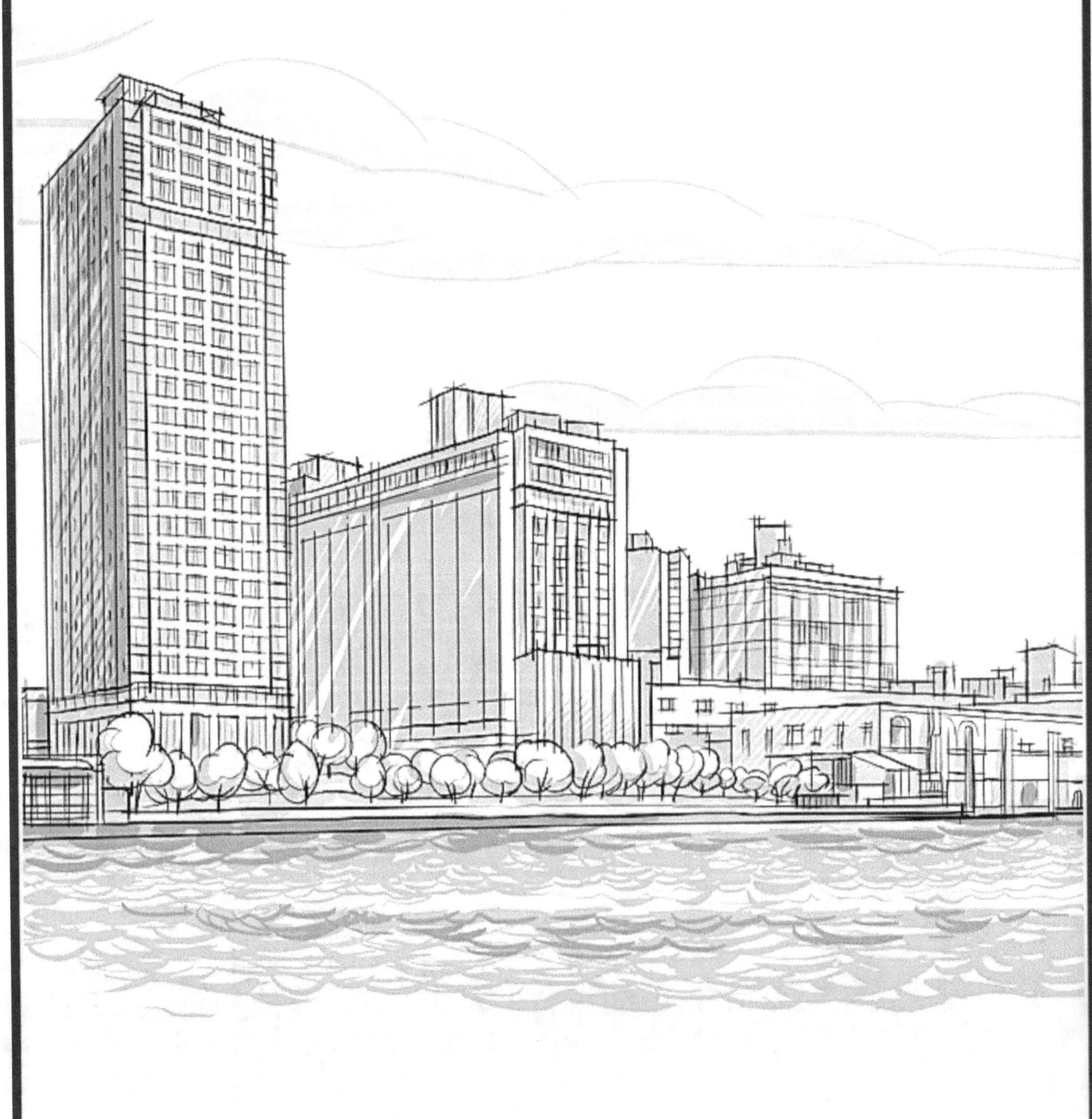

SKYSCRAPERS MALBUCH

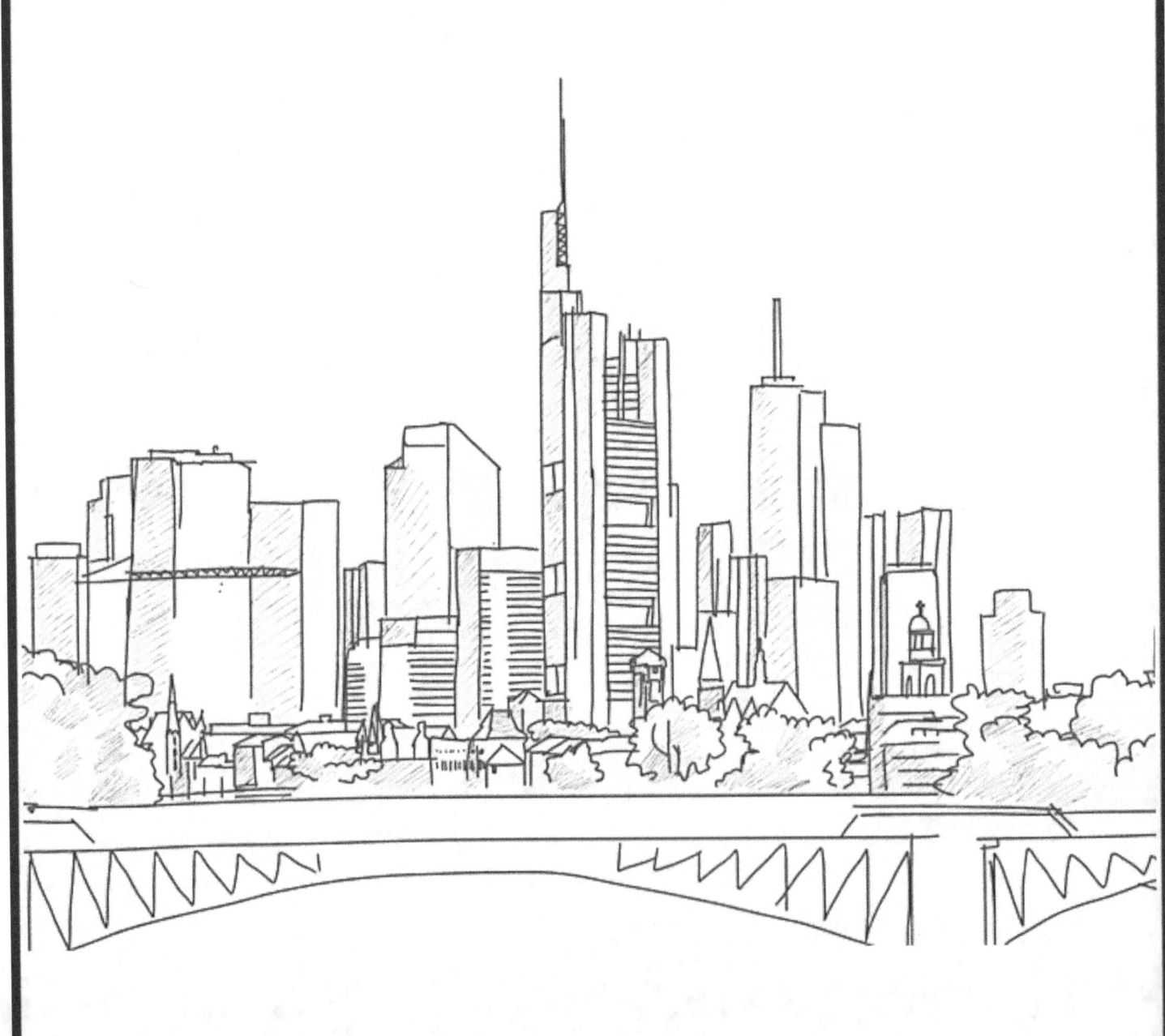

www.ingramcontent.com/pod-product-compliance
Lightning Source LLC
Chambersburg PA
CBHW081447220526
45466CB00008B/2539